Leave your own Legacy

Godfrey Nji Esoh

Copyright © 2018 Godfrey Nji Esoh

All rights reserved.

ISBN-10: 1732451702

ISBN-13: 978-1732451704

DEDICATION

This book is lovingly dedicated to the memory of Pa Daniel Awah Nangah. Also to the young men and women who wake up everyday with the desire to make the world a better place.

TABLE OF CONTENTS

ACKNOWLEDGMENTS i

FOREWORD 1

INTRODUCTION 5

CHAPTER 1: THE STAR THAT WAS BORN OUT OF ASHES 21

CHAPTER 2: TESTAMENT OF GREATNESS......................................31

CHAPTER 3: WHAT IS SUCCESS?..49

CHAPTER 4: THE SUCCESS CODE..71

CHAPTER 5: SAY GOODBYE TO YOUR EXCUSES..........................91

CHAPTER 6: HOW TO CREATE THE SUCCESS YOU DESIRE 111

CHAPTER 7: BUILD YOUR WEALTH CREATION SYSTEM.........119

ACKNOWLEDGMENTS

I am grateful to the following amazing people for having made this beautiful piece of work possible:

All the friends within my social media network who have been faithfully reading and commenting on my essays and have given me the push to compile this book.

Mr. Ngwa Tamu Nangah, heir of the Nangah Estates who authorized me to use the name, portrait, and story of Papa Nangah as the core element of this book; as well as the Nangah children (Ade, Emillie, and Azah), who read the manuscript and gave either encouragement or made vital edits.

My faithful friend and editor Ita Nawom who read every word of the manuscript, polished the language and helped me to fine-tune some of the ideas to make sure my message was clear to the target audience.

Finally, you who are now reading this book. Thank you for joining the community of inspired people. Together, we will make the world a better place.

.

FOREWORD

My spiritual transformation has been taking place over the entire course of my lifetime. But it came to a climax in 2014 when my mother died. Amongst the many transcendental experiences I have been having since then, there is one that stands out - I attended my own funeral. This experience came in the form of a vision in which I found myself in non-physical form, hovering over the congregation that had jammed my local church at Njimafor-Mbatu in Bamenda, Cameroon. There was a cascade in front of the sanctuary with my body in it. The sanctuary was teeming with priests who had traveled from far and near to be part of my funeral. One by one people went to the pulpit to deliver their eulogies.

From my vantage point, I could hear and see what was going on in that church and at the same time, I could have a direct experience of how the event was resonating with the spiritual dimension I was now a part of. It was as if the company of angels and ascended beings were keeping score of which of my earthly achievements had an eternal consequence. Everyone who took the microphone had something to say about the extraordinary person and great achiever I was. If it was an exam, I would have graduated from earth with an A+. yet, on the other side, the score-keepers just stared blankly at me.

I had scored no point. None of my earthly credentials and accomplishments mattered. My life had been wasted. I woke up to find myself lying on the floor, my body shaking. I had sat on the carpet praying and sobbing and asking God "why" because my mother's passing had shaken me to the core and caused me to start questioning everything about life once again.

I stumbled on The Power of Positive Thinking at the age of sixteen. By my eighteenth birthday I had read three other fascinating books; Think and Grow Rich, How to Win Friends and Influence People, and The Story of a Soul. After these four books, I became such a ferocious reader of personal development and spiritual literature that by the age of 33 I had consumed over a thousand books, and recorded significant personal transformation through the application of the principles I learned from them.

What was clear to me from this vision was that I had adopted and built my life on a very materialist view of success. Success to me meant conquering poverty and avenging against the inferiority complex that had plagued my childhood. With my sound academic profile, an enviable career, impressive travel record, and privileged social status, it was apparent that on the other side of life, my mother was more a successful person than I was. Yet this was a woman with no education, no job, no titles, no class. My perception of life changed, and with it, my purpose in life changed.

Over the three years that followed, my African spiritual tradition, Christian philosophy, scientific background, and personal experience into a new and unique model of life which I called "The Success Code". The

Success Code became the new lens through which I perceived the world and assessed the people that the world brandishes as successful people. It became obvious to me that the alarming rates of depression, suicide, heartbreaks, corruption, discrimination, racism, all forms of extremism, war, and famine were all the result of human greed, inspired by a flawed paradigm of success.

This scripture hit me like lightning, "For the creation waits in eager expectation for the children of God to be revealed" (Romans 8:19). I saw the world as a desolate land inhabited by seven billion gods who were oblivious of their divine identity, had no idea of the glorious destiny they came here to manifest and were instead groping around in the dark irking a survival as mere mortals. It dawned on me that the only legacy worth living on earth is not to be counted in terms of bank accounts, estates, certificates, awards, and achievements, but in the number of hearts that one has touched and brought to life.

I became possessed with the new passion of being an inspiration to the world because it occurred to me that although the world was noisy and flashy on the outside, it was dead asleep on the inside. Looking for people whose lives mimic the success code, and shining the spotlight on their legacy as a model of success to the world is one of the ways in which I am now fulfilling my calling. This is how this book came about.

INTRODUCTION

I am writing this introduction in a month that is dramatic beyond measure. It is August 2018, the month in which family and friends in Cameroon and around the world commemorate the 28th anniversary of the passing of the legendary Daniel Awah Nangah, fondly called Pa Nangah. In this same month, as Africans would say, four Iroko trees have fallen in the forest: Kofi Anan of Ghana, former secretary general of the United Nations; John McCain, the war hero, senator, and presidential candidate who has been celebrated as the soul of America; Aretha Franklin, the celebrated songwriter, singer, and pianist who became known as "The Queen of Soul"; and Joseph Kadji Defosso of Cameroon, one of Africa's greatest industrialists.

I was the eighth out of ten siblings born to an uneducated and unemployed village housewife whose husband was already in retirement, had no house of his own, and had no pension, by the time I came into this world. At the age of eight, I accidentally discovered, through a prize award ceremony in school, that this white chunk of tissue between my ears called a brain contained something that I could use to navigate my way from the slums of poverty to the heights of success and prominence. Long story short, I translated academic success into professional success, translated professional success into leadership success, and by the age of 36 years old, I was rector of a polytechnic, the equivalent of a college president in America.

By all standards, my transformation was a miraculous one. But it did not happen by chance. I know exactly what happened and how my life unfolded from one stage to the next. This is the awareness that fuels my passion to inspire the billions of young people around the world who may be in similar or worse situations than I was 30 years ago. There are spiritual secrets I have learned, there are scientific proofs I have gathered, and best of all, there are uncountable personal experiences I have accumulated and synthesized into a philosophy of life that I call The Success Code.

In the community I come from, there is a name that whenever and where ever it is mentioned, evokes a reaction of reverence from people. That name is Daniel Awah Nangah, my uncle who died in 1990 and whose likeness has never been seen since. Because Pa Nangah is such a shining light, I have decided to paint a portrait of his legacy as a means of making The Success Code more understandable and practical. But before capturing the essence of this remarkable man, I begin with a snapshot of other eleven icons of greatness known to contemporary times, as a means of demonstrating that he was not an accident of nature, but one of a kind of people that live and breathe among us.

The greatest obstacle to the release of your potential is the false assumption that great people are extraordinary and you are ordinary. I make the bold statement that great people are ordinary people who have found ways of releasing the potential that is in them, while little people are instead the extraordinary ones because they are not living the lives they came here to live.

JOSEPH KADJI DEFOSSO

Joseph Kadji Defosso was an ordinary boy born in the mid-1920s in Bana in the West Region of Cameroon. He started off as an adolescent petty trader, selling locally produced cash crops like tobacco. In 1972 he had the audacity to create one of the first brewery companies in Sub-Saharan Africa that was not owned by a colonial. Kadji was one of Africa's greatest industrialists who flourished in a multiplicity of business domains including brewery, manufacturing, insurance, retail, real estate, just to name a few. He was one-time Mayor of his hometown Bana. The government of Cameroon gave him the distinction of Grand Chancellor of the Cameroonian National Order of Valor. By the time he died in August 2018 at the age of 95, Kadji was the head of a group of companies that employed 1500 people. His most important landmark in the lives of Cameroonian youths is Kadji Sports Academy.

FRANCIS YONG

Francis Yong emerged from humble beginnings in Kom in the North West Region of Cameroon. As a young typist, he had the vision of empowering other young people to be able to take advantage of the bright career prospects that typists had in post-colonial Cameroon. He opened a typing school which later gave birth to Comprehensive High School (CHS) Bambui. By the time he died in December 2013, Francis had become a household name in Cameroon and beyond. He was loved and fondly called Bobe Yong or Pa Yong. This Education Entrepreneur was the head of the Yong Education Establishments that included Comprehensive High School (CHS) Bambui, Progressive Comprehensive High School (PCHS) Bamenda, Kom Comprehensive High School (KCHS) Anyahjua, National Polytechnic

University Institute (NPB) Bamenda, and Yong Sports Academy. Through the initiative of this one man, close to half a million young Cameroonians have received quality and affordable education.

MOTHER TERESA

Mother Teresa (Saint Teresa of Calcutta) is among the most successful people known to modern times. As an ordinary nun in a Catholic Convent, her life changed when she saw a vision of the suffering Jesus in a desperate beggar, saying to her "I thirst". She turned her life into a mission to feed the hungry, clothe the naked, heal the sick, and shelter the homeless. Teresa had no personal possessions apart from the clothes she wore, but in 1950 Teresa founded a Roman Catholic religious congregation which she named the Missionaries of Charity. She so efficiently translated her vision into charitable action that by 2012, her congregation had over 4,500 sisters and was active in 133 countries.

The congregation manages homes for people dying of HIV/AIDS, leprosy and tuberculosis; soup kitchens; dispensaries and mobile clinics; children's- and family-counselling programmes; orphanages, and schools. Members, who take vows of chastity, poverty, and obedience, also profess a fourth vow: to give "wholehearted free service to the poorest of the poor". Teresa received a number of honours, including the 1962 Ramon Magsaysay Peace Prize and 1979 Nobel Peace Prize. She was canonized (recognized by the church as a saint) on 4 September 2016, and the anniversary of her death (5 September) is her feast day.

KOFI ANNAN

"He was an ardent believer in the capacity of the Ghanaian to chart his or her own course onto the path of progress and prosperity." These are the words with which President Nana Akufo-Addo declared a week of national mourning to commemorate the life and legacy of Kofi Annan, former secretary-general of the United Nations (1997 – 2006) and 2001 Nobel Peace Prize laureate, who died last Saturday at the age of 80.

Kofi was born in Kumasi Ghana in 1938 and raised under British colonial rule. By the time Ghana became the first African country to break the chains of colonialism and usher the powerful new era of independence in 1953, Kofi was a young Ghanaian who saw the possibilities of change and fell in love with the idea of being a change agent. In a 2003 interview, he said: "I grew up with a sense that fundamental change was possible … I saw that things can change, and I had a sense that I could help change things because I had seen it happen at such an early age,"

Zeid Ra'ad al-Hussein, the UN's high commissioner for human rights, paid tribute to Kofi with these resounding words: "Kofi was humanity's best example, the epitome of human decency and grace. In a world now filled with leaders who are anything but that, our loss, the world's loss becomes even more painful. He was a friend to thousands and a leader of millions".

BARAK OBAMA

Barak Obama was not only a black boy raised by a white mother in Hawaii. He was also the product of a broken home. Obama graduated from Columbia University in 1983 and went to work as a Community Organizer in Chicago. In 1988 he enrolled in Harvard Law School where he became the first black president of the Harvard Law Review. Upon completion at Harvard, he worked as a civil rights attorney and as a law professor at the University of Chicago. He rose in leadership to become a young Senator, and when the opportunity presented itself, he grabbed it and put himself in the spotlight that eventually led him into the White House in 2009 as the first ever black president of the United States of America. When he was awarded the Nobel Peace Prize, it was clear that it was not as a result of what he had achieved, but because of the ideal that his person and his life had come to represent to the world. His two presidential mandates were dramatic in many ways, but Obama's true legacy is the inspiration that he is to the world, and how that inspiration will continue to shape the world in times to come.

BILL GATES

Bill Gates dropped out of Harvard University to found Microsoft in 1975 with his friend Paul Allen. Microsoft became the world's largest personal computer software company and Bill became so successful that he has been featured permanently on the Forbes List of the World's Wealthiest People since 1987. From 1995 to 2017 he held the title of The Richest Man in the World for 16 years. Bill retired from full-time work at Microsoft in 2006 to work full time with the Bill and Melinda Gates Foundation which was founded in the year 2000. Through this charitable foundation, Bill donates billions of dollars to humanitarian initiatives, scientific research, and global health. In 2009 Bill Gates and Warren Buffet founded an initiative called "The Giving Pledge", which is essentially a pledge that they and other billionaires are making to give away half of their wealth to philanthropy.

NELSON MANDELA

Nelson Mandela was a young passionate lawyer in South Africa who leveraged the platforms of community leadership and politics to fight against the apartheid system that had been instituted in his country by the white government. His multidimensional anti-apartheid activities finally earned him a life sentence. After 27 years in prison, Mandela emerged as a new kind of warrior who has committed to ending the racial segregation and all the evil that the apartheid regime had brought on his people, while at the same time leading a peace and reconciliation movement that would ensure that the end of apartheid did not mean hatred and discrimination against white people. In 1994 he became the first democratically elected black president of South Africa. He used his five-year mandate to lay the foundation for a new South Africa and stepped down in 1999 despite massive calls for him to accept a second term of office.

After his presidency, Mandela became a world leader who directly or indirectly inspired, shaped, and mediated major peace, leadership, and governance movements around the world. He spent the latter part of his life leading the Nelson Mandela Foundation whose principal mission was the fight against HIV/AIDS. Madiba, as he is fondly called, is revered in South Africa as the father of the nation. Globally he is recognized as an icon of democracy and social justice and has received a total of 250 honors, including the Nobel Peace Prize. In April 2008, I had a life changing experience when I stood in front of the Nelson Mandela statue at Parliament Square in London that he himself had been invited to unveil. "What man lives to inaugurate his own monument, not even in his own homeland South Africa, but in London?" This is the question I asked myself then, and which I still ask myself today. What is it that turns some humans into gods?

MOHANDAS GANDHI

Mohandas Gandhi was born and raised in India in 1869. He studied Law in London and lived a rich professional and political carrier in South Africa and India. He was a ferocious activist against the excesses of British colonial rule. He had the unique ability to assemble masses of rural farmers, traders, and other common people to march in protest to heavy taxes and other forms of social injustice. This tactic which became known as "nonviolent disobedience" ultimately led to the fall of the British India Empire in 1947. This former British colony was granted independence in the form of two independent states; a Muslim majority Pakistan and a Hindu majority India.

Gandhi remained at the heart of activism when internal conflicts broke out as a result of this independence and partition along religious lines One of his trademark protest tactics was fasting onto death. Because of his ideals, he was assassinated by a fellow Indian at the age of 78. The name Mahatma by which he is famously known is not his real name. it is a Sanskrit title meaning, "high-soul", or "venerable". Mahatma Gandhi, the Father of nonviolent civil disobedience was a major inspiration behind the civil rights movement in the United States and the anti-apartheid movement in South Africa. His birthday, October 2nd, is celebrated in India as a national holiday, and worldwide as the International Day of Nonviolence.

MARTIN LUTHER KING JR

What most people do not realize about the household name Martin Luther King Jr is the fact that this phenomenon of a man lived for just 39 years. He was born on the 15th of January 1929 and was assassinated on the 4th of April 1968. Martin Luther King Jr was a Baptist pastor who was inspired by his Christian faith and the nonviolence philosophy of Mahatma Gandhi. He dedicated his youthful energy and eloquent tongue to becoming the voice of the civil rights movement in which he led many nonviolent protests across the united states and gave several moving speeches against racial and social discrimination in the United States.

He delivered his famous "I have a Dream" speech during one of such nonviolent protest outings, "The March on Washington" in 1963. He was awarded the Nobel Peace Prize in October 1964 for his efforts in combating racial inequality through nonviolent resistance. Many monuments have been erected to the memory of this man whose days were few but whose impact will last forever. Hundreds of streets have been named after him, a county in Washington State has been dedicated to him, there is a Martin Luther King Jr Memorial in Washington DC, and Martin Luther Day has been a national holiday since it was enacted into Federal Law in 1986 by President Ronald Reagan.

TOMY ELUMELU

Tony Elumelu is a successful Nigerian banker and entrepreneur who is translating his wealth and career success into a movement for development that the African continent has never seen from one man. Established in 2010, The Tony Elumelu Foundation (TEF), is now the leading philanthropic organization that is championing entrepreneurship and entrepreneurs across the African continent. The Foundation's long-term investment in empowering African entrepreneurs is emblematic of Tony Elumelu's philosophy of Africapitalism, which positions Africa's private sector, and most importantly entrepreneurs, as the catalyst for the social and economic development of the continent.

Through research, strategic partnerships, and its flagship program, the TEF is leading economic and social change across the African continent. Launched in 2015, The Tony Elumelu Foundation Entrepreneurship Programme is the largest African philanthropic initiative devoted to entrepreneurship and represents a 10-year, $100 million commitment, to identify and empower 10,000 African entrepreneurs, create a million jobs, and add $10 billion in revenues to Africa's economy.

OPRAH WINFREY

Oprah Winfrey was born to a poor teenage single mother in rural Mississipi in 1954. She was molested during her childhood and early teens and found herself pregnant at the age of 14. He son died as an infant. The scars of poverty, sexual abuse, racial and social discrimination, teenage pregnancy, and the trauma of losing her baby did not cause Oprah to feel sorry for herself and reduce her life to drugs, prostitution, crime, and other self-destructive tendencies as people would expect of an average person under such circumstances. Oprah rose to become a TV talk show host, actress, entrepreneur, and philanthropist who has inspired millions of lives across the world. She became the richest African American of the 20th century, she became North America's first black multibillionaire, and she was named America's greatest black philanthropist in history.

Oprah became so famous that it is recorded that her endorsement of Obama between 2006 and 2008 resulted in over one million votes that contributed in propelling Obama into the White House as the first black president of America. She later received the coveted Presidential Medal of Freedom from President Obama, as well as two honorary doctorate degrees from Duke University and Harvard University.

THE WORLD AWAITS YOUR OWN LEGACY

There is a common thread that runs across the lives of all these people, and all great people who have lived before them. They are a testament to the timeless truth that people are not limited by the place of their birth or by their surrounding circumstances, but by the size of their vision, the depth of their faith, and the creative work of their hands. In this book, I have zoomed in on the life of one of these legends, Pa D.A. Nanga, the one I knew in person because he was my uncle.

The success principles you will find in this book were not derived from observing successful men and women such as those mentioned in this book. No, I am only using the lives of successful people to validate success principles that are scientific. In the past, people relied on trial and error to find the things that worked and those that did not. Those that succeeded became models for their disciples. The problem with trial and error is that you will never live long enough to repeat all the mistakes that others made before accomplishing what they accomplished.

The problem with discipleship is that copying someone rids you of the opportunity to be your authentic self. Also, since you can never replicate the unique personality and circumstances of the person, the chances of getting the same results are very slim. Creating a system of success based on scientific principles takes the matter outside the realm of superstition and uncertainty and places it in the realm of exactitude and systematics. If you understand the principles, you can apply the methods in your own unique affairs and get your own unique version of success.

I was born into a traditional African family with very strong roots in African spiritual tradition. As a Roman Catholic Christian, I took a keen interest in philosophy, spirituality, and theology, although I resisted the idea of going to the seminary and becoming a priest. I later received the best quality education available in Cameroon in the sciences and worked for fifteen years as a pathologist, lecturer, and higher education administrator.

For twenty years I have been passionately searching for the answers that give my life a meaning, and while doing so, I have been leading thousands of young people at all levels to find and express their authentic selves. The success principles I teach therefore are so unique that you will not find them in any library in the world. They are grounded in the wisdom of African spirituality, proven by modern scientific discoveries, and validated by my personal experience and those of the great people I write about, such as those in this book, and notably, D.A. Nangah.

What all great people have in common is that they have mastered the ability to rise above the primitive instinct of merely surviving, and the egotistic need to achieve great things for the sake of personal glory and have hitched their souls upon that glorious star that guides them to live for something greater than themselves. They put God first as the essence of their being, put humanity second as the purpose they are here to serve, and put themselves last as the instrument that is here to glorify the eternal by serving humanity. Their thoughts, words, feelings, and actions are not inspired by their carnal desires (though they are human) but by the eternal principles of truth, justice, and equality.

Great people are not perfect people who live blameless lives. No, they are imperfect people have lots of weaknesses and make lots of mistakes. The difference with them is that they are always the first to point out their own imperfection and to remind the world that any good that comes out of them is the work of grace. What makes them great is their humility and accepting their weakness and their unique ability to transform their personal struggles into a force for good.

Although we a prone to elevating and quoting the great people who have gained prominence in world history, it is not the prominence that makes them great. The qualities they embody can be emulated and manifested anywhere by anyone in any circumstance. I am living proof that my mother Regina Kieng Nji who had no education, no job, and no status, achieved greatness as a housewife, mother, and member of the Mbatu community. Today, you will not find a street named after her or a monument in her honor, you will not see any TV program about her or read about her on Wikipedia, but there are countless people who will testify to you that she is the star within their soul. Let this be your assurance. You can recreate your life and leave a legacy where you are right now. By so doing, you may rise to prominence if it is your desire to do so. But without money and fame, you can still be great.

If you are reading this book as one of those who are already rich, then take this from someone who has once been a poor kid who like most poor kids grew up being emotionally traumatized by relatives and neighbors who thought that because they had made it in life, other people were supposed to lie on their bellies for them to walk on them. One of the central themes of this book is the redefinition of success as can be clearly seen in the lives of the people cited in this section and in the success code that you will see later on in this book.

If success to you means a distinguished degree from a prestigious university, a high paying job or a thriving business, a fat bank account, a luxurious home, flashy cars, media coverage, women and other fancy things, then you have not even started. It is my mission to make those people who glory in money to become miserable until they put their money at the service of a higher purpose. It is my mission to inspire people who don't have money to free themselves of their limiting beliefs and get both the money and the value that makes people truly great.

The reason why most people read inspirational books and benefit nothing from them is that they read with their heads rather than with their hearts. They are too eager to find that formula that they can just apply and get magical results. The bad news is that such a formula does not exist, and any book that claims to have such a formula is simply lying to you. When you read an inspirational book, what you need to do is forget yourself and your mental stereotypes for a while and allow your heart to flow into the spirit of the book. It is in this way that you become one with the spirit behind the words. The power that inspired the author to write the book becomes your power, the experience of the author becomes your experience, and your life is changed from within.

The secret that will change your life is not found in books, sermons, seminars, pilgrimages, prayers, religious observances, cults, rituals, certificates, jobs, anointed hands, or whatsoever you are looking up to that is outside yourself. All external systems are only instruments which become useful only if they succeed in stirring the sleeping giant within you to awaken and take charge of your destiny. At the core of your being lies that mystery that is variously called the secret place, the kingdom of heaven, the hidden treasure, the Christ, or the higher self. It is this power within that holds the key to unlocking your unknown potential and propelling your life to undreamed-of heights of self-actualization. Inspiration is the art of awakening you to this inner power and showing you how to tap into it. Inspiration is, therefore, the greatest gift a person can ever receive, and the greatest gift a person can ever give.

Lack of inspiration causes people to live from their ego, their only moral compass being the satisfaction of their animal desires. It is this fallen state of humanity that is responsible for loneliness, fear, anxiety, depression, addiction, and suicidal tendencies that affect people in their personal lives. It is this fallen state of humanity that engenders societal ills like discrimination, corruption, racism, tribalism, nationalism, religious extremism, war, and all the other excesses that continue to turn this beautiful planet into a desolate place.

It is due to lack of inspiration that writers, singers, actors, designers, painters, directors, and producers waste away their precious talent at the service of sex, violence, drugs, and horror, rather than channeling it toward painting and praising the best that is in humanity.

Science, religion, politics, education, economics, philanthropy, governance, diplomacy, activism, and all noble human ventures at their best can only patch up external wounds and engender short-term solutions. Inspiration - the illumination of human souls, is the only way to heal the world and return humanity to the sublime reality for which life was created.

The great people you have just been introduced to were not born great, nor did they have greatness thrust upon them by accident. None of them was born into a wealthy home. Few of them were highly educated. Some were white, and some were black. Some were born and raised in America, others in Africa and others in Asia. They all were familiar with personal struggles like hunger, unemployment, homelessness, heartbreaks, and self-doubt. Many experienced tragedies, sometimes coming face to face with death. None of them started life with plenty of capital, special connections, or important family names. In every sense, they were men and women like you and me, who sometimes endured hardships that are hard for some of us to imagine. They rose from the ashes and weaved their unique experiences into beautiful stories that elevated them to the stars.

Now they are shining upon you to challenge you to wake up, stop existing and start living.

The story of D.A. Nangah and all the icons we will ever talk about is your story. The success principles outlined in this book is the roadmap that you can use to move from where you are now to where you can be. Every great person was once an ordinary person like you. One day, something happened that caused a shift in their mentality, after which they took certain steps to shape their destinies and leave the legacies that they have left. Today is your own "One day", as you read these words. Can you hear your legacy calling you? Will you allow the change to happen?

CHAPTER 1

THE STAR THAT WAS BORN OUT OF ASHES

It was a Thursday morning in the summer of 1989. I was inside a sandpit in the valleys of Azo-minyeh in Mbatu Village. I used to spend the summer holidays with my maternal grandmother Bertha who taught me how to channel the water flowing from the heavy rains on the hills to 'wash' sand and sell. I was mesmerized by the white Range Rover that drove by on the earth road beside our sandpit. Everyone knew who it was, for Nangah was not only one of the few car owners in Mbatu at the time, but perhaps the only owner of a Range Rover in Bamenda town at the time.

The Range Rover was driven by its regular driver, the handsome, neat and elegant Joe. Nangah could be seen seated in the owner's seat with a scarf around his neck over his simple jacket. I looked on while my grandmother chanted praises to the great Nangah, and I looked on till the Range Rover disappeared into the other side of the hill, in the direction of Nangah's village cottage at Ndzeng-Bementah below the Mbatu Fon's Palace.

Nangah was my billionaire uncle from my father's side. He was a regular presence in my childhood, but every time I saw him, I was overcome by a feeling of adoration as if in the presence of a god. Standing in that sandpit and watching his Range Rover disappear in the distance, I had no conscious ambition of one day becoming like him. My childhood conditioning had programmed me into believing that such people fell out of the sky and that poor folk like us were poor because it was our destiny. But all of that changed along the way, even without me realizing it.

He and my father, William Nji Tamu, were first cousins. In their days, the word 'cousin' was not known in the Ngemba dialect that is spoken by the Mbatu people, nor was there any allusion to it in our family tradition. In our tradition, to this day, your cousin is your brother/sister and your uncle is your father. Nangah and my dad grew up together, my father being the older brother and him the younger.

My father was born in 1926 to Chi Mbindaga, son of Nji Tamu, while Daniel Awah Nangah was born in 1929 to Monica Bih, daughter of Nji Tamu. The two had gone through childhood adventures together, beginning with carrying firewood, fruits, and vegetables from Mbatu village to sell in Abakwa town. This was in the days when the city of Bamenda was at the now Old Town Bamenda, and the present day Commercial Avenue was only a footpath.

When they became teenagers and were old enough to work, they became yard boys and houseboys for the British colonial administrators at Up-Station Bamenda. Because of their honesty, cleanliness, hard work, humility, and eagerness to always do more than expected, their employers grew so fond of them that they took them along to Nigeria when they were going on transfer.

It is in Nigeria that these kindhearted employers, out of gratitude for their selfless service and as a means of empowering these Mbatu boys to work better, sent them to school. Because of multiple transfers, my dad did just three years of primary school, but the English that this Standard 3 dropout speaks even till date will amaze everyone who comes in contact with him. Nangah had the luck of completing his primary education (Standard 6) before returning to Cameroon.

While working as a clerk with the Public Works Department (PWD) he made friends with people like Kilo who were already established building contractors. It is here that he discovered his natural gift – construction engineering. Through this network, Nangah had his first contract to construct the North West Cooperative Building in Bamenda. He had no capital, but he did something ingenious. Nangah went home to his native Mbatu village and assembled all his brothers, friends, and neighbors who were technicians. He sold to them the dream of using this opportunity to establish a company that will become so big that they will have permanent lucrative jobs and go down in history as the team that would erect glorious buildings in all parts of Cameroon.

These local Mbatu technicians like the builder Joseph Zancho, the plumber Francis Mbah, and many others bought into Nangah's vision, packed their tools, and went to Abakwa town and erected that building on credit. When the contract money was paid, the workers were paid, a new engineering mastermind was formed in Mbatu, and the efficiency of the project won them the reputation and credibility that launched the Nangah Company business. This is where the Nangah legacy begins.

With only a primary education to his credit, Daniel Awah Nangah built an empire that made him the wealthiest person in Anglophone Cameroon. 28 years after his death, no Anglophone Cameroonian has come anywhere near his legacy both in money and good works. It keeps beating my imagination how a man can be the wealthiest man in the land even after 28years in the grave.

Nangah offered scholarships to more young people than anyone can remember. It is alleged that in his day, all you needed to do was find your way into his presence with an excellent GCE results slip and he would toss you into a university abroad with the same ease that your mother sends you to fetch water from the village stream. The interesting part is that he did not limit his largess to his family or village. People who worked for him and had smart children became automatic beneficiaries of his scholarship scheme. When I was in university I had a humbling experience when a classmate bowed to me after finding out that I was associated with the name Nangah, all just because of what Nangah had done for his father, a Bakweri man from the South West Region.

The elegance with which Nangah spent money was the type that would make anyone like to get rich. His palace at Njimafor and his village cottage at Nzeng-Bementah in Mbatu village were open to all. Even though he rolled in Cadillacs and Range Rovers, he was a simple man who treasured little things. It was a blessing to be chosen by your mother to be the one to go and give a basket of boiled Cassava or the local dish Achu to Pa Nangah on a Sunday. Every kid in the neighborhood who had a playmate in the Nangah residence was entitled to royal birthday parties and family outings including swimming in the pool of Sky Line Hotel. Christmas and New Year were always excuses for a free for all party in his compound.

Out of his pocket, he constructed roads, bridges, schools, churches, and health centers. The ring road from Nahkah bridge toward Chomba village, across the entire length of Mbatu village, up through the

Mbatu Fon's palace and back to Mile 90 Nsongwa was dug by Nangah's Caterpillars free of charge. If you have ever gone up to the site of the Fourteen Stations of the Cross that is now a diocesan pilgrimage center, or if you have ever visited the Mbatu Dam, then you may have crossed the bridge at Ntengafor that Nangah constructed almost 40 years ago and which belongs to a class of its own in terms of engineering design and strength, compared to all the bridges in Bamenda. That bridge actually has an expansion line on it to make room for expansion and contraction during seasonal changes.

It is Nangah who founded the Mbatu Cultural and Development Association (MBACUDA). MBACUDA remains the nucleus of the social and cultural life of the Mbatu people today and has kept a track record of executing a developmental project almost every year, in the spirit of Nangah. What most Mbatu people do not know is the fact that it is Nangah's MBACUDA that has been used over the decades as a prototype for the cultural and development associations we find in almost all villages in West Cameroon.

Nangah constructed a private water catchment at Bamendakwe to supply potable water at his residence at Njimafor-Mbatu, near the former Youth and Sports school (CENAJES) Bamenda. Without request or pressure, and without asking for a dime from anyone, Nangah supplied free water to the people in and around Njimafor.

Nangah turned the world into his backyard and made a name everywhere he went. He was a member of the Cameroon Economic Council, he owned shares in and sat on the boards of some of the major corporations of the nation, such as PAMOL and Cameroon Shipping Lines. His Brewery company NOBRA is best remembered by those who were old enough to drink beer in the 1980s. But those who were kids then probably remember Orangina and Marinda. Residents of Limbe all know SONARA and its residential quarters named after him "Cité Nangah", but most probably don't know the story about the man who constructed it.

Nangah owned and ran a postal service that distributed mails around the whole of West Cameroon. The Bamenda Modern Bakery remains engraved in the memories of those who grew up eating Nangah Bread and cakes. The Sky Line Hotel that used to tower over Bamenda town from its strategic location at Up-Station Bamenda was one of the town's landmarks.

Nangah also had another company called Nangah Produce Company which was essentially the distribution outlet of all the cooperative societies in West Cameroon. Through this network, Nangah became the major seller of all the coffee and cocoa that was grown in this part of the world.

Nangah's construction company which he created in 1962, with headquarters in Buea, erected buildings that 40 years later still look more modern than those erected by 21st Century Engineers. Examples can be seen at Clerk's Quarters Buea, the University of Buea (originally ASTI), University of Dschang (originally FASA), University of Douala (originally ENSET), the train stations in Kumba and Douala, the Douala International Airport, Government High School Mbengui, Government High School Nkambe, just to name a few.

When Nangah and his friend Frederik Mubang decided to build a church at Njimafor, they constructed a rock solid stone building and complemented it with a modern presbytery that was decades ahead of its time. Thanks to the availability of this infrastructure and the patronage of these extraordinary men, Archbishop Paul Verdzekov selected Njimafor to host the Italian missionaries of the Sons of Immaculate Conception that later founded the Queen of Peace Parish Njimafor. This parish was inaugurated on March 24th, 1990 and Nangah died on August 31st, 1990.

Nangah was the backbone of the creation of the Social Democratic Front (SDF) which ushered in multiparty democracy in Cameroon. This party emerged out of a monthly Njangui that he and his friends had in his house, all of them being great men who had business and professional interests to protect. This is the reason why this mastermind empowered the courageous Ni John Fru Ndi to stand as the sacrificial lamb and public face of the party. The SDF was officially launched on May 31st, 1990, exactly three months before Nangah's death.

If we call to mind the interesting fact that it is Nangah who opened the bushes at Nkwen and built a house for the retired Prime Minister of West Cameroon, John Ngu Foncha in the place now known as Foncha Street, we will realize that Nangah's involvement in national life did not begin with the SDF.

I do not see the inauguration of the Queen of Peace Parish, the launching of the Social Democratic Front, and the death of D.A. Nangah all in the year 1990 as a coincidence. When you connect the dots in peoples' lives it usually leads you to a fairly clear idea of their destiny. By crowning his life with these two achievements, he seemed to be saying that his work on earth was over. He had built a spiritual fountain that would nourish souls forever. He had served as a principal actor in redefining the destiny of Cameroon as a nation. What more could a man live for? What more could a man wish for?

It is alleged that for every contract Nangah did for the government, he left a caution in the National Treasury as a guarantee. If anything went wrong with the building before the warranty period he gave, money from that caution would be used to do the repairs. I believe that this is true because several years after his death the money that the government paid to his family as part of the debt was enough to make a whole village rich.

Many people claimed that no man could be as rich as Nangah without being a criminal. But after several years of all sorts of legal investigations and tax settlements, there is no bank that has a legal suit against Nangah for unpaid loans, and Nangah does not owe a Franc to the government. It is after all these things had been cleared that the government started releasing money to the Nangah's family, not in millions but in billions. And that was sixteen years after his death. I remember it vividly because former Nangah company workers were called up and paid their pensions and people like Pa Francis Mbah changed the roof of his house out of the joy of such a hefty settlement in his old age.

I was 10 years old when Pa Nangah died at the age of 61. Much of my childhood experience of him did not mean much to me then. It is when I read Robert Kiyosaki's "Rich Dad Poor Dad" that it dawned on me that his story was indeed my story. My good and hardworking biological father is the Poor Dad in my life while my wealthy uncle Pa Nangah and the other super-successful people around me are my Rich Dads. That is how I made the decision that inheriting poverty does not mean I had to remain poor. I could become rich by learning from my Rich Dad, Pa Nangah. Pa Willy, or the Lagos Boy, as my father is fondly called (we just celebrated his 92nd birthday), is poor not in the sense that he is wretched. He is a poor man when compared to his brother, but in another context, he would be a king.

What is the morale of this narrative? There are many dimensions to it for those who have the eyes to see. But I will do a basic summary as follows: If your excuse for mediocrity has been the idea that you don't have certificates, come let us ask Pa Nangah. If you have accumulated bachelors, masters, and doctorate degrees and are still struggling to put bread on your table, come let us ask Pa Nangah. If you have amassed millions or billions and are using your money to feel like a small god instead of doing good, come let us ask Pa Nangah.

This book is written not so much to praise Nangah but rather to elevate him as a shining light to this generation and generations to come. As you can see, it is not a biography. It will take a thousand pages and hundreds of contributors to even begin to do justice to the legacy that Pa Nangah built on this earth over the span of 61 years that he lived. Perhaps it is the overwhelming nature of such a task that is responsible for the fact that till date, his official biography has not been published. This book is about the little I knew about the man from personal experience, the narratives of my biological father, as well as the lore that is associated with the Nangah name in Mbatu village and in Cameroon.

This chapter is the only narrative this book contains. The chapter that follows is a selection of testimonies that came pouring in on my Facebook wall when I published a shorter version of the narrative above. It is then that I realized I did not even know the man I called my Father. As far as I am concerned the following chapter is the best part of this book. It is the outpouring of real testimonies from real people who had real encounters with Nangah. Read for yourself.

Today is the only day left among all the days that have ever been. Today is also the first day among all the days that will ever be. What meaning you make of all the days that have been, depends on what you do today. What quality you give to all the days that are yet to come depends on what you do today.

CHAPTER 2

TESTAMENT OF GREATNESS

On the 7th of July 2018, as part of my inspirational essay series which I publish periodically on my social media platforms, I published a shorter version of this write-up on Pa Nangah. At the time of writing one month later, this article has been liked 224 times on Facebook, shared 61 times, and attracted 180 comments.

In scientific research, there is a method of conducting qualitative research that involves the use of focus group discussions to collect data on a subject of interest. A focus group is a small group of usually seven or eight people that are systematically selected by the researcher to represent the population he/she is studying. A good research study will usually conduct three focus groups, and then pool the results to construct new scientific knowledge based on themes that emerged from the guided discussions.

Facebook creates an open discussion forum for random participants to read and comment on my articles. I have 5000 friends on Facebook and more than 2000 others that are connected through my personal groups and pages. Friends forward my articles to their friends, who in turn have the opportunity to take part in the discussion. The way Facebook works is amazing. You never really know who is going to read something you have posted. In many ways, the random selection process of Facebook is more reliable than the one we try to do physically when we are doing field research.

The article under discussion provides a focused talking point such that it is easy to keep track of the various angles and observe how the different inputs weave themselves into a common theme in real time. Why am I bothering you with this introduction to research methods? Because I want you to notice that when 80 randomly selected people participate in a coordinated discussion on a specific question, then what we have in hand is the equivalent of qualitative data generated from 10 to 15 focus groups. That means that if we apply the rigorous process of analyzing these comments and constructing themes from them, we would have created some new knowledge through a process that is scientific, knowledge that provides an answer to questions that bother us.

In the rest of this chapter, you will find some of the striking comments that people wrote on my article about D.A. Nangah. Most of them are tributes to this great man, but many contain pointers to the following questions:

- Who are we and what is our purpose on earth?
- How do we know we are fulfilling our purpose - what is success?

- How do we go about fulfilling our purpose – what is the secret of success?
- What are we leaving as the legacy by which we will be remembered when we are gone?

We can use this data to validate a theory of success that I have developed from my 20 years of research and experimentation on the subject. "The Success Code", which you will see later on in this book, presents a model of holistic success that anyone can use to redesign their lives. My short portrait of the legacy of D.A. Nangah may have moved you, but what will move you more is what other people say about D.A. Nangah, most of them people I have never met.

Noel Chuye Tangko

What a narrative!!! I knew of many of these ventures but would never have believed just one individual was behind them all. The interesting thing is that his legacy is still very solid to date.

Grace Unending

Wonderful write-up sir! I wish you had taught me this in school instead of bacteriology and immunology. On a second thought, I guess it was all part of the process. Let's keep this light burning

Genevieve Bi

Wow, this is spectacular. Didn't know much about the old man but this is quite admirable. We have a lot to learn and not even a 10th of it involves sitting in a classroom.

Achiri Atanga

Thank you so much, bro. You awaken a lot in me via this post. Thanks again. Keep motivating us.

Valery Nji

Nangah was a one-man army in Mbatu and the whole of Cameroon at the time. Whenever I visit the famous old CENAJES and Nangah Street named after D.A. Nangah, I still see his mansion standing tall amidst the recently constructed houses. In fact, he was a man of quality. I remember vividly the famous Nangah Bread which had quality compared to none. Even today's bread cannot measure up to the quality his bread had at the time. He was an icon and his legacy still lives and shall continue for generations to come.

Muma Bih Yvonne

An understatement to qualify his "standard six" certificate as "ONLY". This gentleman was more than ten Ph.D. holders put together. He had our nation and most especially our North West Region at heart. Forever green in our memories.

Julius Nji

Very correct, I went to Catholic School Njimafor Mbatu which he constructed and was fortunate to be a friend to his sons: Taku Nangah (of late); Ade Nangah somewhere in the US, Nji Nangah in the US; Awah Nangah in UK and Ngwa Nangah in Cameroon (the next of kin. The legacy of Late Pa Nangah is clearly visible.

Tang Smith

At first, I thought the story was too long for me to finish, but I only realized I need more to read.

Junior Ekins

I agree with you, Pa Daniel Awah Nangah was indeed a great man. His legacy lives on because he invested in the wellbeing of his people. I did not know him personally, but so many of us benefited from his benevolence. He constructed the Health Center in Ndagh-Mbatu which was later used as the original building of a new school, Government Bilingual High School Mbatu-Bamenda, a school that has educated thousands of children including me. That's a classic example of "Strive not to be a success, but rather of value to society" (Albert Einstein). Excellent write-up, thanks Goddy!

Muma Bih Yvonne

I have always nursed the thought of a foundation or memorial in honour of this Legend. Your write-up is an eye-opener. Cannot wait for such an initiative to be launched. I hail you Godfrey Nji Esoh.

Mel Melanie Gwandua

Wonderful lesson. My dad used to say that a man like Nangah is hard to find. His intelligence was unspeakable despite little or no education.

Kelly Fogwe Tayim

Great narrative and thanks for sharing. I had the opportunity of knowing Pa Nangah same year he died, correct me if I am wrong. After writing one of my best GCE O-Levels papers -Geography at Presbyterian Secondary School Mankon in 1990, I went out of campus to get some puff-

puff and beans at our usual spot Mama and Papa Fonebi Palm Wine Bar. I saw this beautiful strange American car parked outside. As I ordered my food and was eating, little did I know that it was Pa Nangah sitting next to me and drinking palm wine with Pa Fonebi. He ordered Mami Fonebi to give me more food and drinks and took over my bill. I was very sad to learn of his death that same year. But what he did to me on that day has stayed in my mind forever. My experience goes a long way to confirm this write up.

Budi Nji

Our Billionaires of today rather make money on the sweat of the common man by evading taxes and hiding under the canopy of the ruling party. You find them contribute hundreds of millions to support political campaigns but would not contribute a dime for village development in their communities. They can't provide even potable drinking water for their people talk less of building a classroom for children studying under trees.

Rex Tayong

Come to Mutengene and I will show you many families that he enriched around that region. My father - a Mbatu man - was one of them. Blessings.

Emille Nangah-Alintah

Godfrey Esoh thank you very much. U wrote knowledgeably about my father. Yes, he was a father to everybody. He used to tell me this *"Big Mami, God no give me all this money for me one.* He gave me wealth to help others." His firm belief was that you take the money you need, and use the rest to help others. Mr. Godfrey Esoh, thank you. God bless.

Sabi Pikin

Proud to be born of this great man I called my father. RIP Daddy.

Geraldrico Gúevara

Great man...amazing!! We seem to have lost all the great and good people!!

Frank Zanche

My brother, I have tasted part of Pa Nangah's glory and there is no exaggeration in your narrative. I grew up in Cité Nanga in Limbe. The tennis court and the basketball field are just amazing. When I got there because of my auntie who recently retired from SONARA, I wouldn't hesitate to ask about the whole complex and I had a proud answer *"Na Bamenda man build this place"*. When I went to Mbatu for a burial in 2008 and saw that palace you have mentioned, I was thrilled before I was given the same Limbe answer *"You no know Pa Nangah he compound?"* My brother, you are very right and I am very proud of Pa Nangah.

Che Dieudonne Tabong

My mother always says in family meetings; "work hard with ethics like Nangah. Even if you die, your family will remember you when spending your money."

Mosken Ndeh

His compound in Njimafor Bamenda built in the 1960s has stood the test of time. We are still hoping to have people build and live in houses like that by 2045.

Sally Mulumba

His story should be taught in schools. He was a dear friend of my dad's and a husband to my aunt. Though I never met him personally I have heard a lot about him. My dad's narrative is similar and from him, I learned the power of giving and blessing others. Leaving a legacy is important.

Ngum Ngafor

Yes! Examples from our own society. Love it!

Nchang Angelinafombu

He was a good man wonderful father and a nation builder.papa may u soul rest in the lord

Fred Takum

Thanks for sharing this summarized biography of Pa Nangah. That's one man who inspired so many persons. I had a personal experience with him when I was as a kid. Our neighbor, a taxi driver, who was carrying us to Nkwen, crashed Pa Nangah's Range Rover around the Bamenda Hospital Roundabout. The taxi driver came out and lay prostrate on the tarred road crying. He knew that even if his Renault 4 taxi was sold, it would never have been enough to repair that Range Rover. Surprisingly Pa Nangah came out and helped the taximan to his feet, comforted him and gave him fifty thousand Francs to go repair his taxi. His magnanimity taught me at that early age, a lesson I will never forget.

Jovita Nsoh

He was a true legend. He deserves monuments and streets to be named after him.

Fon Fru

Very excellent write-up, thanks for inspiring us with memoires like. The only thing I Can say about him is that when he died, his compound in old CENAJES was packed with people. I was still a kid then, but I heard everyone speaking good of him, and till today they still do.

Ejong Ndelle

Hi Goddy, Just to let you know my late dad was one of the many Southern Cameroonians who benefited from Pa Nangah's scholarship scheme. He eventually emerged as an entrepreneur, following the steps of Pa Nangah. The legacy of Pa Nangah will never be forgotten. May his soul rest in peace.

Bih Evangeline Mbom

Wow, this grand-uncle of mine was really a role model. I was not fortunate to see him as he died when I wasn't born yet. But I've heard so much about him that is so inspiring.

Aloysius Mbako

One of the best and most pragmatic entrepreneurs of his era and not still equaled. Yes, Pa Nangah was rich but he did not work for mere riches. He was proud to build the best with the best engineers and business people around him and from all over the world including Americans, French, British, Italians, and even Russians. He compensated his entourage down to the drivers and housekeepers in a way that motivated them to do their best possible. Mr. Nangah would not stand for mediocrity and would go to any extent to produce the best buildings etc. I witnessed him deconstruct whole buildings just from suspecting wrong proportions of concrete or the slightest structural defects.

This is a Cameroonian who proved that our country could produce businessmen of world quality. I still meet with his former chief painter, a Frenchman who is now retired in Paris. He still holds Pa Nangah in the highest esteem as an entrepreneur who amazed his European, American and Russian engineers by his thoroughness and his insistence on quality. That's what makes us so proud of a man whose life should have been much longer to assume other leadership positions we so much lack. I don't know about school but certainly, Pa Nangah worked with the mind of a knowledgeable man capable of analyzing complex business matters. That's what education is. He was above all a pragmatic man to the core.

Hilary Chi Ndikum

Powerful. Well-articulated. Nangah will forever remain my greatest icon. Chi Béton Construction is working hard, praying fervently and striving to the utmost, to emulate Nangah Construction Company.

Hilary Chi Ndikum

I'm really humbled bro. Thanks a lot for sharing the life and works of my greatest icon. He was really one of a type. I will live to be meditating on this great write-up.

Nzeh Valentine

Very interesting and educative. That is our anglophone culture. If all these embezzlers and rogues had emulated Nangah's example, Cameroon won't have been like this today. Thank you Mr. Esoh for citing that example. People should always think positively.

Melanie Mayonghe Kesiki

Wow Goddy. I grew up to hear many things named after Nangah but didn't really know he was such a great man. Thanks for celebrating him. We need to celebrate our heroes. We don't need people to help us sound their fame. From this story, we've got many lessons to ride home with. Once more thanks Goddy.

Sylvester Ndeso Atanga

Yes, this is the honorable Dan Nangah himself. Cameroon Government was not fair to this visionary. He lives forever in those of our minds who knew him. I met and discussed lively several times with him in his best friend's house the Late Dan Che when I just returned from Uncle Sam's Country. Che was another business magnet at the time with a near similar background. We will forever have fond memories of them.

King Bobo Adille

Wow! Wow! I can only challenge myself with the question, "what can I not do?

Kate Akoachere

Nation building means everybody owes his country and deciding to love your country back. Nangah is an epitome of grace and generosity who was sensitive to the needs of others. How I wish we also do the same and build our nation so that the country will move forward. All hope is not lost. RIP, dear dad. You will forever be a hero.

Taku Claude

He is a great man even in his grave and his legacy reigns forever. A lot to learn from this icon

Love Takor

Don't like reading long articles but this one got all my attention. Good write up Godfrey Nji Esoh. We shall be the Nangah's of our generation. God bless.

Patricia Nwantoly

I only saw him from a distance but from the stories I heard, Goddy you have correctly presented his legacy. Pa Nangah's death was a big loss to the Mbatu community in particular and the nation in general. My family had just moved to Nangah street a year before he died but I quickly learned about his kind-hearted nature in less than no time. For example, while the government public tap poured out water that was almost the colour of tea, Njimafor and its environs had clean water the quality of Tangui water to drink. Our street (Nangah Street Njimafor) was one of the few private roads that were tarred in the 1980s, all thanks to him. Death took him too soon but he left an amazing legacy. May he Rest in Peace.

Ndong Elias-ivor

I am very impressed with this write-up with summarizes the marvels that Nangah's life represents. I remember how he built that Mbatu Integrated Health Center fondly called "Maternity" by the villagers of Mbatu, Nsongwa, and Chomba that were served by this health facility. I remember how he fought for the creation of the government secondary school which is now Government Bilingual High School Mbatu. I was the first batch of this school.

I have never forgotten the sensation of shaking hands with Professor Joseph Mbui, the then Minister of National Education when he visited our school. It is Nangah that constructed the Bamenda Main

Market. All his structures stand out as masterpieces compared to the standards of his day, and even today. On the evening before the day he died, a rainbow appeared in the sky and we saw a star fall out of the sky. My dad told us that a giant would die. We woke up the next day to hear about the passing to glory of Pa Nangah.

Prudentia Akum

Wooh! A rich man with a golden heart. Very handsome too. Nice write-up brother.

Khayi Loveline

Your write up is just sooo beautiful it drove me to tears, my dear Godfrey.

Samuel Kum Zih

I have never heard of this nobleman before, but his story is one of a kind. It is so rich and inspiring.

Muma Bih Yvonne

Another idea springs up in my mind after scrolling through this outpouring of testimonies. Godfrey, please make sure you collect and save these and more to serve future generations, some of whom have indirectly benefited from his legendary largesse without knowing.

Ikome Ngale Speaks

Even though I didn't meet him personally I grew up in Bamenda where his name was everywhere back in the 1990s, especially his generosity. What a Legacy.

Wally Senior

I grew up in Limbe and remember the joy we had each time we went to Cité Nangah. I remember the National Karate Contest for kids in Cité Nangah in 1992 where I won a yellow belt. Memories of my five years studies in the University of Buea are still fresh, talk less of my exploits with Godfrey my super buddy from Njimafor- Mbatu. Nangah has directly impacted my life. May his soul rest in peace.

Abanda Jones Bahfri

The article is well written but it gives just an iota of the largesse of Pa Nangah. I never knew he did not have a college degree but I remember (if my memory is correct) he was awarded a posthumous "masters in construction engineering". He is was a great man and a very big great man.

Ngia Nche

Growing up in Bamenda I heard many good things about Pa Nangah. He was so wealthy that the lazy and wicked started questioning his source of wealth. I also heard he was a very generous and devout Catholic Christian.

Jovita Nsoh

I also want to add that Pa Nangah (Ngia Awah, like we fondly referred to him) was, by and large, the father of multiparty democracy in Cameroon. Although not widely publicized due to business implications (at the time), he played a major role in the founding and financing of the Social Democratic Front (SDF). Unfortunately, he died shortly before the success of the return to multiparty politics. The SDF recognized him by marching straight to his grave in Njimafor on the day multiparty system was restored in Cameroon.

Carene Sabum

Wonderful piece. Pa Nangah was my dad too because I grew up and interacted with all his children who took after their father in the area of kindness and generosity.

Evg F H Banks

Thank you sir Esoh for this masterpiece. I'm indeed so challenged. True riches are for outreach, the number of souls you touch. Anything less only makes you a wretched millionaire.

Nchem Rudolf

He was the richest Cameroonian according to Cameroon Year Book 1976 to 82 when Paul Biya took over as president.

Bessike Paul Amedee

I grew up in Limbe and have always enjoyed going to Cité Nangah to visit friends till today. I equally studied at the University of Buea and I can say that those buildings were definitely not only beautiful but solid. In fact, most of the super-rich people I have known in Cameroon were not University degree holders and usually hardly were they educated. Finally, this is very inspiring.

Victor Etta

Truly an icon in Cameroon entrepreneurial milieu. My personal recollection of him can be traced back to the chantiers where my dad Chief John Ebai Etta served as the chief engineer and Managing Director for Nangah Company contracts at the Dschang University and CAMSUCO sugar factory in the mid to late 70s. I am forever grateful to Mr. Nangah for personally recruiting my dad from Nigeria and showing him the ropes for him to eventually establish his own building construction company in the early 80s. I can still picture them both parading the sites of their chantiers,...commanding giants as they were,...indelible imagery of my perception of what I aspired to as a child in the late 70s. They are both gone now, but their legacy is forever with us. Thanks, Mr. Esoh for sharing the story of this most important influential Cameroonian icon with us.

Steve Njoke Molua

I have always been digging research information about this man. Alongside his legacies, he built SONARA Nangah Quarters and so many public buildings. He was a real estate guru in West Cameroon. Long Live his soul.

Fayez Nduku

Robert Kiyosaki's "Rich Dad Poor Dad" is the book everyone should read. Here is a real example right in our own home. What are we waiting for? Waiting for heavens to open the gates? We've got to start some strategic thinking and wise implementation of the so many skills we have acquired.... I love this Nangah story. What a motivation.

Ailicec Chinyere Nangah

So proud to call him my daddy! Keep resting dad! Godfrey Nji Esoh such a great tribute! I didn't even know he built all those buildings! He died 10 days after I turned 9. But I hold on to the little memory I have of him.

Amabo Comfort

O my G!!! What inspiration!!!! I knew very little about Pa, but I must say I'm amazed by the picture of all the above buildings constructed by him. Nevertheless, I indirectly felt his touch through his wife Ma Nanga Elizabeth.

Doris Ngum

Interesting analysis that takes me back to my childhood in Pa Nangah's compound. Wealth is within everyone and waiting for relevant strategic actions.

Loh Benson

The man with the Baritone Voice! He brought me from Douala to his Sky Line Hotel Bamenda in 1984. It is there that I started my journey to stardom. Thank you Pa Nangah! Your spirit lives on.

Fomo Mbinkar

I don't know this man, but his name I do. Godfrey, you owe Cameroon the duty to put such a man's life in a more detailed and comprehensive book for future generations to savor. Great write up. I read it with a lot of interest

Noel Chuye Tangko

Definitely; Godfrey Nji Esoh you need to put this great man's life in a more detailed and comprehensive write-up. Finally, there is (yes, I am using the present tense) someone in my hometown who compares with the likes of Andrew Carnegie, Henry Ford, and Thomas Edison.

Victorine Ngah

He lives forever in our minds.

Life begins to have a meaning only when you begin to live for something greater than yourself. He who transcends self, rises above race, religion, politics, culture, nationalism, and all the divisions that hold human souls captive, even time and space. He who transcends self, becomes a god.

CHAPTER 3

WHAT IS SUCCESS?

Before I introduce you to the success code, I will use this chapter to give you a brief rundown of the philosophy that forms the basis of the success code. The reason why less than 5% of human beings ever come anywhere near the fulfillment of their vast potential is that over the ages man has been pursuing success but has hardly ever taken time to define success. Imagine stopping a taxi and telling the driver "Go". He will drive until his gas will get finished and you will still not be at your destination because you don't have a destination, to begin with.

Let me warn you that the content of this chapter is deeper than you expect. We live in a world that is so superficial that people will gladly allow someone else to brush their teeth for them. So when you want to talk about success people are just eager to hear the secret – the how. They have no time to dig deeper into the source of things and master the why. Unfortunately, nature does not specialize in short-cuts. Humans keep trying that and they keep failing. Those who become masters and gurus like Pa Nangah are people who take time to go to the source. When you master the "why", you gain the power to create your own "how".

There is a general perception among Africans that in order for a man to distinguish himself from the masses, such as in the accumulation of great wealth or the attainment of great heights in career or political office, such a man must dabble into some cultic practice. As such, every great person is often looked at with suspicion. This suspicion in itself justifies the poverty of the onlookers because they tell themselves that the reason why they are poor is that they do not engage in such practices. But let me tell you upfront that the reason why some people are rich and others are poor is that the rich know certain things that the poor do not know, and do things in a certain way that the poor do not.

It is mental laziness on the part of the poor that causes them to look for excuses to justify their condition. If you summon the courage to read this chapter to the end, you will accept with me that there is no way you can know these things and still go about looking for powers whether in churches, shrines, or secret societies. It is all in your head. What churches, shrines, and secret societies do is that they teach you at most one-tenth of these truths and coach you into putting them into practice while hypnotizing you into remaining faithful to them because you think they are the source of your power. Read, reflect, read again, apply, and see for yourself.

We live in a universe in which everything unfolds following a specific pattern. The electrons circle round the nucleus of an atom, the moon circles around the earth, the earth circles around the sun, the sun circles around the Milky Way galaxy, and the Milky Way galaxy circles around the galactic core. These cycles give rise to the sequential unfolding of days, nights, and seasons, which in turn determine the periods for planting and harvest, and the mating seasons for biological life.

From breathing to heartbeat, menstruation to gestation, from sleep to death, everything in the human experience unfolds according to specific patterns. Whether it is in the structure of DNA, the shell of a snail, the unfolding of the fern plant, the formation of sand dunes in the desert, the hurricane, the orbits of electrons, moons, planets, suns, and galaxies, the same toroidal geometry or pattern of motion is visible. Now we also know that even as these patterns are made manifest in the physical universe, time itself unfolds in cycles, such that our current age is a strand on a cycle of time that predates documented history.

The scientific evidence is overwhelming, that rather than being a chaotic soup that bubbles by chance, the universe is a matrix that is holographic and fractal. The laws of gravity, electricity, motion, and all other laws that science has decoded as being responsible for the formation and manifestation of the universe, only go to add credit to the fact that the world we live in is not happening by chance. The laws of mechanics are so precise that we have used them to land man on the moon, and plant satellites on distant planets.

If the laws, or our interpretation of the laws, were to be inaccurate even by a fraction of a second or millimeter, the satellite would miss its orbit and come crashing back to earth. If the universe was a chaotic mass that had no intelligence and intention behind it, then one day a cow would have three legs and another day the sun will rise from the south. That the universe moves in a specific pattern that accurately replicates itself from the atomic structure to the galactic structure and everything in between, is an indication that there is a code for this movement.

Nowhere else is the idea of coding more apparent in nature than the genetic code that we find in biological life forms. Every biological life form is the phenotypic or outward expression of a genotype or genetic code. The genetic code is a sequence of base-pairs contained within the nucleus of an organism, that gives instructions to the organism about which amino acid molecules to synthesize, thereby controlling the processes of growth, differentiation, repair, and metabolism. Each species is defined by a specific genome which we commonly call DNA. The genome varies in complexity from the unicellular amoeba to the complex human being.

Within each species, each individual is defined by specific sub-variations within the genome. A code is, therefore, a system of symbols that set the blueprint for the expression of a message or phenomenon. It is from the idea of a coded universe that man came up with the idea of computer codes. Every computer program is simply a system of codes or symbols that uses programming language to give instructions or commands for specific outputs. The staff notation on a piece of paper is a code for the music that can be decoded by a pianist, the same way the solfa notations can be decoded by a choir. The architect's blueprints are a code for the construction project.

It is obvious that a code is a symbolic language that someone familiar with the coding language needs to interpret following specific rules, in order to produce the desired message or output. It takes a builder to interpret the blueprints written by an architect. It takes a musician to interpret the blueprints of a song. It takes an operating system to interpret the blueprints of a computer program. Looking at the sophistication of the various codes in nature and the precision with which the patterns are repeated from the cycles of electrons around the atomic nucleus through the cycles of time, tells us that there is no way life could have evolved by chance.

There is no way the universe could be expressing itself in the absence of an intelligent and intentional force. Our coded universe, therefore, implies that there is an invisible intelligence beyond the visible universe that is coding the universe, a force that is interpreting the code to give rise to the phenomenal universe, and a system of laws or principles by which this interpretation is taking place.

Man has a physical body that is part of the physical universe. Man's body, therefore, unfolds after the same generic patterns that are found in the physical universe. Cell division, growth, repair, metabolism, and death are involuntary functions that are programmed as part of the universe and which are not within the control of man's free will. But man is not just a body. He is a spiritual being having a human experience through the vehicle of the body. While the physical life of man unfolds according to preprogrammed patterns, the spiritual life of man unfolds according to mental processes that he is totally in control of.

A good analogy for this process would be a driver and a car. The manufacturer of the car produced the car following a specific blueprint that determines the shape, color, longevity, speed limit, and other mechanical functions of the car. The driver's duty is to master the parameters within which the car functions, and then freely decide where he wants to go and direct the car to take him there. So long as he uses the car within the set parameters, and does the regular refueling and maintenance, the car will be a faithful servant.

Your physical body is coded by your genetic make-up and the metabolic processes are the mechanics that keep the body functional. You are the pilot that is navigating life in this space-time realm using the vessel you call a body. This vessel is programmed to function optimally for at least seventy years if you fuel and maintain it properly. Its use is to serve you as you journey through this phase of life, using your free will to define and fulfill your purpose for being here.

You are a spiritual being whose life unfolds as conscious processes that occur within your spirit self, are transmitted by your body, and reflected on the three-dimensional space-time screen to produce what your senses interpret as your experiences. Just as the material universe of which your body is a part unfolds according to patterns, codes, or laws, the spiritual universe of which your spiritual self is a part, unfolds according to patterns, codes, or laws. In the visible universe, every life form blossoms to its full potential when its code is interpreted correctly.

When some external force acts on the code and a mistake occurs in the process of its interpretation, a mutation or error occurs. In biological life, these errors manifest as birth defects or diseases such as cancers. In cosmic life, these errors manifest as cosmic accidents like hurricanes, earthquakes, melting of the polar ice, global conflict, and so on. The environment is the force that shapes the expression of biological life, and man is the force that shapes the expression of cosmic life. The correct interpretation of the code, in an environment that is conducive for the expression of the life form, is, therefore, necessary for the life form to express its full potential.

It is the purpose of the mango seed to give birth to the healthiest and most fruitful mango tree that ever was. It is the purpose of the zygote in a woman's womb to give rise to the healthiest and most beautiful human body that ever was. Life is eternally expanding and increasing, reason why every new thing strives to be better and more amazing than its previous version. Since man is a being with a dual nature – a spirit in a body, he also has a dual purpose. His body must blossom into the healthiest and most beautiful body ever seen so that it can serve as a suitable vessel for the human spirit to overflow and enrich the world with the most glorious expression of life ever known.

Everyone wants to succeed in life, but few people ever stop to ask themselves what it is that they call success. We wake up every morning and rush to school or to work and come home exhausted, always looking eagerly to the future but not really clear about what we are expecting. Man's quest for success and meaning is so great that the success industry has become one of the wealthiest industries in modern time. People consume motivational books, tapes, seminars, and retreats almost like drugs, and yet this thing called success still eludes more than 95% of the people who study hard, work hard, and pray hard for success.

Those that are really successful in our world are so few that we have given them names; stars, heroes, gurus, great men, extraordinary women, and so on. We forget that what they have achieved is what is normal for all of us. By worshiping them and calling them extraordinary, we have normalized mediocrity and considered success a rarity. In simple terms, success is the efficient and effective realization of the predetermined goal for which a thing was made.

The goal for which an apple seed exists is to grow and blossom into a fruit-bearing apple tree. The goal for which your iPhone was made is to help you make and receive calls and help you live your life better by managing all the smartphone applications installed in it. The goal for which a human being is created is to illuminate and enrich the world with the most magnificent expression of the divine that can be channeled through the human form. Everything is channeling the divine in its own way; the galaxies, the suns, the planets, the earth, the seas, the birds, the flowers and trees; everything is the divine source overflowing into expression.

The channeling of love, mercy, compassion, beauty, wisdom, creativity, abundance, and joy, through the human experience, is the purpose for which man lives, his physical body being just the vehicle for the creation and sharing of these states. We, therefore, must thrive in body, in mind, and in spirit. We thrive in spirit by allowing the divine source within us to flow. A dam that has no exit becomes a hazard. But when it is opened up, the resulting stream brings life to the valley through which it flows, and the dam remains fresh and alive.

We thrive in mind by rightfully using our mental faculties. The right use of the mind is to illuminate it with the awareness of the divine essence within, saturate it with the knowledge of the inner attributes, and guide it toward being a channel for the outpouring of the springs of living water from within.

We thrive in body only when our spirit and mind are thriving. When we are living from the divine source within, the mind becomes a river of life that flows freely and abundantly, the body, like the banks of the river, teems with life, health, freshness, beauty, and our affairs (relationships, work, finances, etc.), flourish like the valley that knows no season.

The paradigm of success that the world has been pursuing for centuries is actually the reason why many lives are so miserable. The first problem is the false premise that man is a physical being that is separated from the divine, the cosmos, and fellow man. This premise claims that man is inherently empty, poor, unholy, and undeserving of the good he desires, and so must earn what is needed for his wellbeing through effort, which may take the form of physical, religious, occultic, mental influence, or law of attraction practices.

The success teachings we have been used to consuming, therefore, approach success from this false premise, and teach success as an achievement which may be gained through the application of the endless variety of techniques that are developed and taught every day. How can you change your life simply by manipulating your thoughts, words, feelings, and beliefs? The teachings themselves prove their own weakness. If you can influence your beliefs, then have you ever stopped to ask who is the power behind the beliefs and how does that power form those beliefs?

Your life is a tree. Your self-concept or identity is the sap or life within the tree, your beliefs are the roots, your thoughts are the trunk, your feelings are the branches, your words are the leaves, and your actions are the fruits. The identity you ascribe to yourself determines the quality of beliefs, thoughts, feelings, words, and actions that spontaneously flow from you. If that self-concept is limiting, your life will be a hell, no matter what you do on the outside to change it. If that self-concept is expanded, your life will naturally be fruitful and joyous.

Transformative success is, therefore, the true path that your life should take. If you find your authentic self, define your purpose in life, and get busy living that purpose, the universe will orchestrate itself to surround you with all the good that corresponds with this expanded experience that you are giving to the world.

Even my unschooled grandmother in the village knows that in order for you to get a bag of maize, you need to prepare the fertile ground and sow a handful of grains. But in our modern world, we wake up and run about like bush animals running away from a wildfire, in pursuit of jobs, money, relationships, social status, physical appeal, and so on, in the hope that when we have these things we will then feel successful and start living our life's purpose. Since when did the harvest come before the planting?

You are a divine seed planted in the garden of earth with the purpose of germinating, growing, and manifesting the glory of the Infinite Spirit that is breathing through you as your life. Just as each flower contributes its blossom to create the magic of the garden, just as each star contributes its magnificence to make up the magic of the sky, so too are we here to each contribute our greatness to make up the magic of earth.

Is it not written in scripture that the world groans as with the pangs of childbirth, yearning for the manifestation of the sons of God? Did Jesus not teach us to pray "thy kingdom come; thy will be done on earth as it is in heaven"? We are the seeds of heaven, scattered on this earth to blossom into the glory of our father thereby bringing heaven to earth.

Of course, life is eternal and there are universes within universes and heavens within heavens, so bringing heaven to earth does not exclude the possibility of the higher state of heaven after life on earth. What is certain is that the end we wait for will never come for us if all we do is fast, pray, and wait for some rapture or judgment. If the universe is consistent in its laws, and we agree it is, then every life form is bound to fulfill its purpose. Man's purpose is to express the divine life through the human vessel, thereby establishing the kingdom of heaven on earth.

Your quest for health and fitness, love and romance, work and money, success and recognition, happiness and longevity, is the natural urge of the life force within you. There is no difference between that which you seek and that which is depicted as the Garden of Eden or the Promised Land in the Old Testament, and the Kingdom of Heaven in the New

Testament. The state of bliss in which you are fully alive in spirit and mind and prospering in body and affairs is what heaven really is. Its only variation is its expansion in scope as the soul ascends into deeper and deeper union with its source.

We read in 3 John 1:2 that "Beloved, I pray above all things that you prosper and be in good health even as your soul prospers." The apostle prays for your prosperity above all things. But here is a twist, your health and prosperity are conditional on the prosperity of your soul. In Matthew 6:33 Jesus sets the golden rule of success in these words, "seek first the kingdom of God and his righteousness, and all these things will be added onto you". I like to be in a place where I don't need to work for money because money is being added onto me; where I do not need to spend sleepless lonely nights gripping my pillow, because love and companionship is being added onto me; where I do not need to go under the doctor's knife or travel to attend a healing crusade, because health is being added onto me; where I do not need to sacrifice all that gives me joy because of my job, because abundance is being added onto me. How about you?

When Jesus talked about the kingdom of God in this context, he was not referring to a place you go to after you die. I can prove that to you. The things he said will be added onto you if you are living in the kingdom, are clothes and food and all the earthly things we worry about. In this discourse, he challenges us to learn from the birds of the air and the lilies of the field which do not worry and toil but are better fed and better clothed than Solomon in all his glory. Is it not a mockery of the very idea of God to suppose that he cares more about birds and flowers than you?

Jesus is asking you and I "are you not more than these birds and lilies, oh you of little faith?" Faith is defined for us here as seeking the kingdom of God and dwelling in it, such that our lives become the river of righteousness (right standing), that naturally causes our body and environment to blossom. If this kingdom is not a place we enter after we die, then it is surely a state of consciousness we enter into here and now. It is a spiritual identity we acquire here and now.

The gospel writer Mark puts these words in the mouth of Jesus as the opening phrase of his ministry, "The time is fulfilled, and the kingdom of God is at hand: repent, and believe the gospel" (Mark 1:15). The phrase at hand is wrongly translated and we assume it means "near". What Jesus actually said is that "The time is now fulfilled, and the kingdom of God is now here: turn away from your old mindsets, therefore, and believe this good news."

The good news is the spontaneous overflow of heaven through you to shower the world with love, joy, beauty, abundance, and goodness; if you turn your consciousness away from the paradigm that has kept you trapped in suffering and regret, and become aware of the kingdom of heaven that is now here as you, waiting for you to let it flow out then success is an effect of your happiness, not the cause of your happiness.

The divine essence that is within you as you is the truth (the source of all that is), the life (the fullest expression of truth which you call success), and the way (the mechanics or secret by which truth manifests itself as life). Your primary concern in life, therefore, is not the search for success techniques by which you can do, but the alignment of yourself with the laws of success, the being state called righteousness. It is from your 'being' that your 'doing' flows. When the being is right, the doing is effortless and joyful. And all your good is simply added onto you.

Since 2008, August 19th of each year is commemorated by the United Nations as World Humanitarian Day, to pay tribute to aid workers who have risked and lost their lives in humanitarian service around the world. On World Humanitarian Day 2012, Beyoncé Knowles staged a song titled "I was here" whose lyrics go as follows:

I wanna leave my footprint on the sands of time

Know there was something that, meant something that I left behind

When I leave this world, I'll leave no regrets,

Leave something to remember, so they won't forget

I was here

I lived, I loved

I was here

I did, I've done, everything that I wanted

And it was more than I thought it would be

I will leave my mark so everyone will know

I was here

I want to say I lived each day, until I die

And know that I meant something in somebody's life

The hearts I have touched will be the proof that I leave

That I made a difference, and this world will see

Since we live in a social media age, I strongly recommend that you search for this song on YouTube. Watch the video and feel the story it portrays, then watch another version that contains the lyrics. Don't just watch – sing along and feel the words as if it was a confession you were making to yourself. This exercise alone has the power to change your life forever; if you just do it.

There is a difference between the rest of the universe and man. The life of all forms and phenomena in the universe unfold automatically according to the patterns that are coded in their embryonic states. In man, this spontaneous unconditioned unfolding of the life force is conditioned by the state of consciousness that man occupies. Man is the image of God in the sense that within the physical body is contained the real man, who is essentially the breath of God, or God-individualized. Individualization or Free Will has only one obvious purpose; that of 'specializing' the creative principle that unfolds in a generic fashion in the rest of the universe.

If all mango seeds produced identical mango fruits and all human seeds produced identical human beings, then life would be a boring recycling of the same thing. But God in his infinite wisdom, after creating this generic universe of identical types, created the human form, clothed himself in it, and entered into this creation, so that through this fresh platform called Individuality (You), he could replicate the same creative process by which he brought forth the generic universe.

Replicating the universal creative principle on an individual scale affords a mechanism through this generic principle is specialized. The result of specializing or conditioning the universal creative principle through our free will, is a personalized universe. The specialization of the universal creative principle through the agency of individualization or free will guarantees the infinite variety of expression which we term "the glory of God".

Yes, since God is Infinite Potentiality, a mechanism for Infinite Expression is a necessity within his being. Generic laws run to a conclusive end because they are fixed and predictable and the best they can do is produce an identical cycle. Individualization (God's own image existing within creation), makes it possible to specialize the law and create a new personal universe anywhere, anytime, thereby guaranteeing continuity, expansion, and excitement. By this token, man is a spiritual being housed in a physical body living in an expanding physical universe of which he is a co-creator.

To help us understand this concept better, let us use the metaphor of a computer game. The computer programmer is a creator. He writes the codes for a computer game following the exact script he has in his mind for each character in the game. If you play that computer game a zillion times, you will always get your results within the scope of predictability set by the computer codes. So, while the computer game makes for good entertainment, it is simply the recycling of the same script, and it eventually gets boring.

Now, imagine that this creator has the means to breathe a piece of himself into a chosen species of characters within the computer game, such that each character now has the ability to replicate through its own free will, the exact process that the creator underwent to create the computer game. He (the living character) has the identical capacity as his creator, his only limit being that he has to exercise that capacity while trapped in a body that is part of the matrix of the computer game. So long as the universe of the computer game is concerned, this character is a god.

What will obviously happen now is that the game will experience a dichotomy. The elements that are generic will continue to respond automatically to the codes, while the individualized character will now have the power to introduce its own commands to influence how the original commands play out in its experience. The introduction of an individualized consciousness within the field of Infinite Consciousness produces the divergence called personal experience, which culminates in the infinite self-expression of God that would not have been possible without such a specializing agency called man.

Man is the son of God in the sense that man is God's image of himself in the universe. The son and the Father are obviously one in essence, only different in scale. And since the son is truly the Father wearing a human form, anyone who sees the son, sees the Father. The son is the Father in human form. You are not here for life to happen to you. You are here to create your own version of life. As your Father has life in himself, so has he granted you (the Son) to have life in yourself, and the way for you to live your life is to do as you see your Father doing.

God is spirit. Spirit is pure unconditioned energy. Spirit is the source of all things. Spirit creates by becoming that which it contemplates itself as. Man is spirit. If self-contemplation is the means by which Spirit creates, then self-contemplation is the means by which man creates. That which you know yourself to be, you are. When a grain of corn is planted, it just grows and bears more corn. It does not go to school to learn how to germinate. It does not attend motivational seminars to learn how to grow leaves. It does not fast and pray to beg for grains from heaven so that it can produce ears of corn. All that it needs to become the best yielding crop, is contained within the seed in the form of its genetic code that is read by the life force to bring that potential to fruition.

The problem with man is that since he is a free spirit, his self-contemplative activity (thought process) interferes with the spontaneous unfolding of this life force through him, such that the outcome is not the automatic result coded in nature as is the case with the non-human life forms and phenomena, but the personalized version that has been conditioned by the quality of thought that is going on within him. The consciousness that is buried in the ego can only produce suffering because the ego is nothing but the accumulation of experiences generated through the senses and the socially constructed myths that the person ends up calling his identity.

When the consciousness is immersed in the ego, it sees itself as a limited self that needs to succeed, a hungry self that needs to be fed, a naked self that needs to be clothed, a homeless self that needs to be sheltered, a lonely self that needs to be loved, a poor self that needs to get rich, a weak and oppressed self that needs to survive. This false identity gives birth to a paradigm of life as a race for survival through effort, competition, and conflict. The success philosophy of the ego identity is "do something, have something, be something". So, the typical approach would be to figure out how to make more sales so as to get more money so that I can be happy. The popular success teachings are founded on this paradigm of man as an emptiness that needs to be filled through the application of techniques.

It doesn't matter by what fashionable names the various teachers call their systems. Whether they are training you to be a better salesperson, motivating you to think positive thoughts and speak positive affirmations, coaching you to visualize and feel good, or mentoring you to repeal and replace your beliefs, all of them are variants of the same childish "give me, give me, give me" mentality. It also does not matter if these teachings come in the form of expensive retreats in hotels and cruises or in the form of sermons from pulpits.

As our spirits lie buried in the Golgotha of the ego and the life force is continually being poisoned by the toxic clouds of self-centeredness; mediocrity, failure, disease, misery, conflict, exhaustion, depression, and death are inevitable. When the consciousness becomes aware of itself as the living spirit rather than the ego and its experiences and awakens to the reality of its oneness with the Infinite Spirit that gives rise to all, permeates all, and contains all, the sublime self is born.

The sublime self is aware of itself as the absolute, eternal, and infinite spirit living in a human body for the purpose of expanding life through the use of free will to specialize the universal creative principle. The sublime self is aware of itself as the fullness of life in the eternal now, which needs to receive nothing from the world but rather needs to pour itself out to the world. The sublime self knows that its life is God-in-essence unfolding as God-in-expression so as to bathe the world in the splendor of love, beauty, goodness, wisdom, power, abundance, peace, and bliss. The sublime self knows that the glory of God is the real purpose of life and that the glory of God is man truly alive.

The sublime self is not preoccupied with what it will eat, drink, or wear. It is rather preoccupied with what the other will eat, drink, or wear because it knows that by converting the fullness of life within him into solutions that bring the glory of life to others, all that he needs for his own wellbeing will be added onto him. The sublime self basically says, "I will get busy taking care of others and let the Father stay busy taking care of me".

To those who are in pursuit of ever-increasing life and happiness for the world, success comes in greater measure than they know what to do with it. To those that wake up daily and wear their running shoes to go out and pursue success, success always flees from them, or when they do get a certain measure of success, it is always transient, or at the cost of something else.

Since your self-contemplative activity is the mechanism by which the life force gets conditioned to produce your experience of life, won't it be wonderful if you had a template for success that your life should look like? The mind is like a schoolboy who runs off to play each time you are not watching. The absence of a template for your thought process and the uncertainty in your mind about what success is for you is the reason why your mind gets seduced by the senses and turns you into a slave to effects, rather than a master of causes.

My contemplations on the key questions of life, my personal experience of life, and my study of every human person I have read about, known, or interacted with, from the ancient Egyptian Pharaohs that were considered incarnations of the gods, to my youngest son that was born on the 10th of August 2017, have led me to formulate a success code that is made up of three core pillars and twelve attributes or traits. The pillars define the person's inner essence while the attributes define the person's outer experience.

The success code is summarized below and elaborated upon in the next chapter. As you read through it, I want you to go back and reflect on the life and legacy of D.A. Nangah presented in the first two chapters of this book and establish for yourself the degree to which his life reflects this success code. This will help you through the mental process of accepting that these are not just abstract ideas but a practical template for success derived from the lives of real people.

I have the unique benefit of having been born and raised in Cameroon in a family with strong African spiritual history and practices. I am highly educated in the medical sciences and have considerable experience in clinical practice, research, and teaching. I am also a fervent Roman Catholic, although I am more fascinated by the rich Christian philosophy and spirituality than by the dogmas and religious ordinances. My worldview, the lens through which my philosophy of life and success is formulated is, therefore, the most unique one. When you interpret Christian philosophy in the light of African spirituality, back it up with the evidence of modern scientific discoveries, and validate it with your personal experiences and those of the people you have known, you come up with something so new that Plato himself will be envious of you.

Now you have the philosophical basis for the success code which forms the core of this book. You may want to come back to this chapter and read again and again till these thoughts become your own. Once you grasp the philosophy (the spirit behind the theories), the theories become your own and the practice becomes natural.

The three pillars of success, the three pillars that make up the inner essence or nature of a successful person are:

- Knowledge of the Truth
- Being the Truth
- Living the Truth

The twelve attributes of success, the twelve traits that a truly successful person should manifest are as follows:

1. Spiritual Awareness
2. Mental Soundness
3. The Emotional State of Joy
4. Physical Health and Wellness
5. Harmony with Nature
6. Fulfilling Relationships
7. Creative Self-Expression
8. Career Excellence

9. Financial Prosperity
10. Positive Social Impact
11. Quality Time
12. Self-Fulfillment and Perpetual Growth

Money, power, and all the physical things we usually define success by are not success in themselves. They are the result of success. Success is like a tree that produces money, power, influence, and all material advantages as its leaves and fruits. If you do not look deeper, you will be chasing the shadow instead of the object.

CHAPTER 4

THE SUCCESS CODE

It is a privilege to present to the world this gift that I call "The Success Code". If the only thing I ever achieve in life is to provide a model by which billions of people can pattern their lives and work toward the unfolding of the glorious destiny that is locked up within them, then I would have served as a messenger for the coming of the kingdom of heaven. Is there any work that is more important than this? I doubt that. If I am to spend the rest of my life teaching just the success code, it will still be the most important job on earth.

As we have seen above, the success code comprises the three pillars of success and the twelve attributes of success. The three pillars of success, the three pillars that make up the inner essence or nature of a successful person are:

Know of the Truth

The Master's directive in John 8:32 states that "You will know the truth and the truth will set you free". Faith begins with knowledge. The only salvation we really need in life is salvation from the insanity we have created for ourselves through the process of social conditioning. The greatest sin, if not the only sin, therefore, is ignorance. When we become aware of the falseness of our conditioned self, only then do we awaken to the truth of our sublime self. When we know the truth, we are indeed set free. But how do you know the truth? The answer is simple; by studying. There is no other way to gain knowledge but through study.

The modes of study vary depending on your environment, but you must study. For me, my study began with the oral tradition that was passed down to me through myths, legends, the folklore of my ancestors. When I became a grown-up Christian, I started digging deep into scripture and the documents of the church to satisfy my curiosity about where the creeds, dogmas, doctrines, and rituals were coming from. Then came my quest for the secret of success that led me to read nearly a thousand books in the fields of self-help, positive thinking, psychology, sociology, education, spirituality, theology, metaphysics.

My career as a medical scientist also helped reinforce my appetite for knowledge because, in the field of medicine and academics, you either read or you perish. Yes, I know what you are thinking. I am a bookworm. My friends used to call me that since secondary school. The good news is that you don't need to be a bookworm in order to succeed in life. I can assure you from my personal experience that it is not knowledge that is power. Real power is the knowledge that is acted upon. So what you need is to identify the area you are passionate about, start looking for books written by authorities in that area and start stocking your shelf. I generally recommend that you set a target of reading a book a week.

Before you complain, let me remind you why you are studying. The person that you now are, was formed as a result of the conditioning you inherited from your parents, the conditioning your mother transmitted to you when you were in her womb, the conditioning you received as a child, and the conditioning you have received from your environment through your education, religion, and personal experience. It has taken more than a lifetime to build the Wall of Jericho that you want to bring down and enter into your promised land. The study of truth is what it takes to disrupt your old conditioning and replace it with the new one that will create your new reality. One book a week is just to help you cultivate the habit of studying. You will eventually get to the place where you will have no use for TV, idle gossip and social media.

Be the Truth

That which we know in the rational mind must become part of our intuitive mind before we are able to experience it. In spiritual language, to know something is to be that thing. That is why it is written in the Bible that no man can see God and remain alive. What that scripture really means is that to see God is to become God and therefore to cease being a mere mortal. When Moses descended from the mountain, that was God himself who had taken the form of Moses, not the old Moses that went up the mountain. The transforming effect of truth occurs only when we meditate on that which we have learned intellectually. God's instruction to Joshua summarizes this principle succinctly: "Keep this Book of the Law always on your lips; meditate on it day and night, so that you may be careful to do everything written in it. Then you will be prosperous and successful (Joshua 1:8).

Again the book of Psalms opens up with; "Blessed is the one who does not walk in step with the wicked or stand in the way that sinners take or sit in the company of mockers, but whose delight is in the law of the LORD, and who meditates on his law day and night" (Psalms 1:1-2). The daily practice of meditation is what we call in academic circles "reflective living". Meditation has nothing to do with weird postures and breathing exercises. It is the simple habit of thinking about who is thinking your thoughts, examining the thoughts and the experiences that create the thoughts, and connecting the dots to make meaning. The reflective life is about always asking "why?". In the beginning, it will be useful to set aside some quiet time when you can be alone in a comfortable environment for a few minutes each day just to meditate. But with practice, meditation will become your lifestyle and you will become a walking meditation.

Live the Truth

Finally, that which we know intellectually (in our heads), and believe intuitively (in our hearts), we must incarnate in our bodies in order for the creative circle of life to be complete. Let us try a little exercise. Right now, decide that you are relaxed and happy and watch what happens. Next, start laughing. Don't think about laughing; don't ask why you should laugh; just laugh for a minute or two. Have you done that? Now notice that you are now actually relaxed and happy. It is the same difference between listening to music and dancing to the music. If you did not do the laughing exercise, maybe the dancing exercise will be more conducive for you. Play your favorite song, get up, and dance your soul out. Then notice how you feel.

Pay attention to what happens in your body when you actually take an action, say laughing or dancing, as opposed to just thinking about it or visualizing it. There is a huge secret embedded in this little exercise. You are a spirit that is living in a body and experiencing itself as a mind. When you create an image in your mind through thinking, that image calls up its corresponding emotion in the heart (subconscious mind). Thought travels on the wings of emotion into the spiritual realm where it mobilizes the creative forces of the universe to bring to you that which you are thinking about. That which the universe sends to you, you will receive through your body, that is, through action. Living the truth, therefore, means taking the action that corresponds with the thoughts and feelings you are having, such that your body and environment will be in alignment with that which the universe is sending to you.

For example, when you are desiring love and companionship, the action to take is to look for someone who desires love and companionship and be the love and companion they need. In so doing, you have opened the floodgates of your life for your good to flow in – the love and companionship that the universe is sending to you. When you are expecting money, the action to take is to take the little money you have, look for someone to whom your little is a big deal, and give it to him. By being the source of abundance to that person, you open up the floodgates of abundance in your life through which universal abundance flows to you.

We can, therefore, sum up the three pillars of success into the head, heart, and hand; or intellect, intuition, action; or mind, soul, body; or simply know the truth, be the truth, and live the truth.

The three pillars of success are like the three stones that make up the fireplace in the African woman's kitchen. When all the three stones are in place, only then can the pot stand properly on the fire to be cooked. The twelve attributes of success are the twelve pieces of wood you need to make your giant fire with which to cook out of life any dish that catches your fancy:

Spiritual Awareness

You are spiritually aware when you have found out through inspiration or suffering that the life you have been living is false because it is the product of your conditioning. When you recognize the falseness of the conditioned self, you become open to the truth of the sublime self that has been sleeping within you. You are aware of a higher power, not because your religion says you should but because you have had a direct experience of the limitations of that which you used to hold as true. You walk by faith and not by the evidence of appearances, not because some spiritual teacher or success coach says you should, but because you have had a direct experience of the reality that all that appears is flowing from that which is not seen.

After all is said and done, when you are given the gift of what some call a holy death, you can rest assured that the Author of life is smiling upon you. Pa Nangah knew months ahead of time that he would die. During his last trip to London, he personally did his funeral shopping, that is, the items with which he would be buried. He took his eight-year-old daughter Azah to the shop and she saw it all, but she was too young to understand then. When he returned home, he took care of business, took care of family, took care of any scores he needed to settle, and planned his own funeral. On the eve of his death, he called the parish priest, did his final confession, received his final communion, and said his goodbye.

That day, the people of Bamenda saw a rare spectacle, a giant rainbow circling the sun. the old and wise knew that a giant soul had left the earth, but none was prepared for the news when it broke. Pa Nangah was no more. While all of this does not prove anything in itself, everyone who was close to Pa Nangah will testify to you that he was one of the most spiritual persons you could ever meet. He did not just profess Christianity; he lived it out loud through his prayer life, his illuminating presence in the Christian community, and his community service.

Mental Soundness

You have become aware that all that is happening to you is not by accident, but that your life is really the broadcasting of the images of your mind. The pain and suffering in your life have taught you the bitter lesson of allowing someone else to rule your mind and therefore decide your destiny for you. You now refuse to swallow everything that is thrown at you by the media, the church, the scientists, the politicians, etc, and really start thinking for yourself. And the substance of your new thought is found in inspired books. So you chose to become a habitual reader of inspired and empowering books, not horror novels and murder stories.

Among his last words to his daughter Azah who was eight years old at the time were these words, "Mama, you see all those houses and property I have? If people come and take them away, or if anything happens to them, I can recreate them from what is inside my head. That is why you should never joke with your education. If you create wealth inside your head, you will always be able to create anything you want". I wish every father could teach this principle to his children when they are eight years old. If we did that, the world would be advancing so rapidly that fathers will not recognize the world their children have created. Although he had just six years of formal schooling, Pa Nangah was one of the most educated people you could find in the land. If you were to award a Ph.D. for each of his major achievements, the man would bag at least twenty of them.

Emotional Security

Because you are deeply rooted in spiritual truth and greatly inspired by true knowledge, you are no longer the helpless cork that is tossed around by the tides of external words and events. People don't annoy you. Bad news doesn't make you afraid. Challenges don't make you bitter. The emotional toxins of fear, doubt, and worry which cripple most humans do not come anywhere near you because they are the children of ignorance, and you are not ignorant. You do not read books, watch tapes and attend seminars that are trying to help you get a positive mental attitude. Positive thinking is not something you do, but who you naturally are, because out of the abundance of faith, hope, and love that you are, naturally flows the qualities of joy, peace, happiness, gratitude, enthusiasm, courage, forgiveness, humility, and goodness.

When you read the testimony of the student who met Nangah in a palm wine bar and he paid for his food and drinks; when you read the testimony of the young man who witnessed Pa Nangah console a weeping taxi driver and gave him money to go and fix his taxi instead of scolding him for having bashed his Range Rover, you know that we are talking about a man who was so emotionally secure that all he ever wanted was to make people feel loved and appreciated. The power he had was not derived from the inflated ego that most rich and famous people have. His power was his humility that caused people to love him and feel at home around him. The children of all the homes around his compound went to his compound to play with the Nangah kids, and when Papa was around, the kids would run to him, rather than away from him.

Physical Health and Wellness

The absence of fear, doubt, and worry in your life means the absence of the greatest of anxiety, the cause of stress which is the mother of all chronic diseases. Through the proper balance of feeding, work, exercise, rest, and recreation, you keep your body healthy, fit, and charming, thereby making it a suitable vehicle for the expression of your greater self. You may be the most gifted singer on earth but what good will that do you if you are always sick? You know that the health of your body is a key component of success.

Pa Nangah was as handsome a man as you will ever meet. He was fit, healthy, and strong because he lived a healthy lifestyle that balanced good nutrition, work, exercise, play, and rest. His only bad habit was his fat cigars. It is lung cancer that deprived this planet of the life of such an incredible man at the tender age of 61.

Harmony with Nature

You are aware that the same elements that make up the cells of your body are the same elements that make up the planet and the stars. In other words, your body is a microcosm of the universe. A crucial aspect of your physical health, mental alertness, and spiritual awareness, therefore, is the degree of harmony that you enjoy with nature. For some people, it is swimming in the ocean or freshwater ponds. For others, it is walking in the woods. For others, it is making sure their diet is dominated by fruits and vegetables. For others still, it is taking occasional walks barefooted. Everyone has their preferred mode of tuning in with the universe. Finding yours and using it to make a daily connection with the whole out of which you emerged, is a key to keeping you in perfect condition.

It is not for nothing that the setting of my narrative about Pa Nangah begins with his Range Rover navigating the earth road among the hills of Mbatu village. Pa Nangah has a certain affinity for nature that people could not explain. He was a wealthy town dweller who had a palace containing every comfort one could dream of, but he never spared an opportunity to drive to the interior of Mbatu village where he had his cottage in the heart of the forest where he had been born. He participated in cultural festivals, funerals, and traditional ceremonies, where he felt at home like an ordinary village man, ate achu, cassava, and roasted chicken, drank palm wine, danced Mbaghalem, and performed the traditional gun firing ritual called Ala'a.

His old cottage in the heart of the forest is still standing there and when I visited it some six years ago I was overcome with a certain feeling that gave me first-hand experience of why he was so attracted to that environment. When you find a place where you can be alone with nature once in a while, you have found a sanctuary where you can retire to reflect, renew your spirit, and emerge as a new person with new ideas to pour out to the world.

Fulfilling Relationships

Love is the nature of the spirit within you. We are products of Unconditional Love, so it is in our nature to give love. Relationships are the avenues through which we give the love that we are, and by so doing allow the other people to give the love that they are. When you are lonely it does not mean that you are not loved; it rather means that you are not loving. Love is what you are, so you don't go around looking for love; you should rather be going around looking for opportunities to love. Different people play different roles in your life and so you express love to each one according to the measure of the role that person is playing in your life. You love your spouse or partner differently; your children differently; your parents and siblings differently; your friends and colleagues differently; and strangers differently; but it is all love. This quality of success is so important in African culture that the African paradigm of success is not about how high you rise above others or how much money you have accumulated, but about how many happy people you are surrounded by.

Whether it was his children, wives, brothers, sisters, cousins, nieces, nephews, church members, community members, employees, or business associates, Pa Nangah had a flair for winning the affection of people. His love knew no social class, no gender, no tribe, no religion, no skin color, no nationality, no political party. He had friends everywhere and was friendly to people of all generations. I was very touched when on one occasion ten years after Papa's passing my siblings and I visited his widow and we sat in her room upstairs looking down at his grave through the window and listened to her talk about her husband as if she had fallen in love with him just yesterday.

The wealthy African king that he was, he was a polygamist. But each of his wives would testify to you that he treated her as if she was the only queen in the world. The bond between the children till date makes no distinction between which mother gave birth to which child. The quality of his human relationships, even in a complex domestic setting set Pa Nangah apart as a truly remarkable man.

Creative Self-Expression

You realize that apart from the formal education you received to earn a certificate, you have a unique story that has unfolded as your life. You embody natural gifts, talents, and skills that make you come alive whenever you are expressing them. These are your superpowers, things you do naturally, spontaneously, effortlessly, and without expectation of reward. When you are expressing your superpowers, you feel like a god. You know at least one thing in your life that your friends and family think you are a genius at. You may not have realized it before now, but it is along that path of these gifts that your true calling is, not in the conventional education and job. You will become more successful when you take inventory of all your superpowers, take time to perfect them and find ways to leverage them. Your success lies in the territory where you are spontaneously expressing your authentic self. If you find ways of bringing your education and job into this romance, then you have hit the jackpot.

The young Nangah was a clerk at the Public Works Department. In his day, that was a white collar job from which he would have retired as a well-to-do man had he held on tight as many expected him to. But he had the audacity to abandon that lucrative, secure, predictable comfort zone and throw himself out into the unpredictable arena of entrepreneurship. The passion for building burned so greatly in his heart that he could not have had peace had he not followed his dream. In his example, we see a clear distinction between having a job and following your calling. In today's society, all that people dream of is to have a job that will bring in a steady paycheck that they can use to clear the bills from month to month.

The Cameroonian public service, for example, is the graveyard of the genius of the youthful generation of today. There are great engineers, entrepreneurs, and inventors that will never be because they traded their potential with the alluring ease of passing an entrance into Training Colleges and securing government salaries as teachers, doctors, and so on. The problem is not the jobs themselves, but the laziness that befalls the human spirit when your account is credited every 28 days with the amount of money that makes you neither rich nor poor, but happy enough to remain where you are. Pa Nangah opted for self-expression, not employment, and that is what led him into wealth and greatness.

Career Excellence

A successful life is measured by the amount of service it renders to the world. When you leverage your specialized knowledge, specialized skills, superpowers, and networks into a service or product that adds value to the lives of others, then you have found a career. The number of people whose lives are made easier, healthier, richer, and happier by your service, determines the degree of success you earn in life, which usually reflects as recognition and money. But by now you already know, that there is a difference between greatness and fame. Not all great people are famous and not all famous people are great. Fame comes and goes at the whims and caprices of Hollywood, while greatness lasts forever, in the hearts of those whose lives you touched.

Can we find any better words to declare that Pa Nangah enjoyed a successful career? Read the first two chapters of this book again and engrave in your imagination what one man's career left for the world. This is what happens when your job coincides with your work or your calling. The majority of human beings work forty hours a week on jobs they hate because they are slaves to their bills. They burn with the desire to release the dream that is within them, but they lack the courage to do so. It does not mean that in order for you to follow your calling you must be an entrepreneur. No, you can choose to be an employee who is doing the work that you are passionate about. It is your authenticity and passion that elevates you to heights of prominence in any walk of life.

Find out what you are gifted at. Determine the industry of career in which that natural gift will thrive, then get to work and convert your gift into a gift to the world. If you do not find an organization that will give you the opportunity to release the genius in you, go ahead and create yours. That is what Pa Nangah did.

Financial Prosperity

You want to be in the place where money flows to you easily and effortlessly through multiple channels in ever-increasing amounts on a consistent basis. It is only when you have financial security, when you have no money worries, that you have the luxury of living life on your own terms. And yes, the whole idea of success boils down to living life on your own terms. When you put money in this context of the Success Code, you suddenly realize that no amount of money is too little and no amount of money is too great. It boils down to the person that is creating value for the money. Do not be deceived by the ones and zeros you see printed on paper. Wealth is in the mind. I can put one billion dollars into better use in Cameroon than Bill Gates has use for 100 billion dollars in America. Mastering the idea of money is a key element of success.

Pa Nangah has plenty of money. He demonstrated that a man can get more money than he can spend on himself and his family for two lifetimes and still have enough to shower goodness on an entire village and country. In his life, we see a radical redefinition of wealth. Wealth calculating ventures such as the Forbes Classification of wealthy people defines and ranks people according to the billions and millions of dollars they have amassed.

Pa Nangah was beyond this childish view of life. It is difficult to hear the name Nangah mentioned anywhere without it being associated with some marvelous work that he did. To him, money was only a tool in his hand. He mastered the art of making it, and he enjoyed spending it to enrich other peoples' lives. I am particularly excited about this subject of money because if you are one of those who defines success only in terms of money, then you now know from the life of Pa Nangah and the Success Code, that your success rate is just one-over-twelve (1/12).

Quality Time

Do you know those people who own million dollar mansions around the world but do not spend as much as a week in them each year? Do you know those parents who do not have time to spend with their kids because they are too busy? How about the lady who lies in bed with her husband and is excitedly recounting her day only to notice that the guy has since fallen asleep? Sounds familiar? If I were to define success in one word that word would probably be "freedom". Part of your success means affording the freedom to enjoy quality time with the people that matter to you, take part in the social activities that matter to you, be an engaged member of your community, travel and see the world, pray, play, dance, and do all that brings joy to you and others. Without this, all other achievements are without meaning.

I sincerely do not know how many children Pa Nangah had. But when each of his children speaks of him, you have the impression that that child was an only child. The man had time for his children. I have mentioned earlier how he was a regular presence in the village either relaxing in his cottage or attending ceremonies around the village. The church he built and patronized was a home to him whenever he was in town. He was known and loved in other parts of Cameroon, Africa, Europe, and America as if he lived there full time. How did he afford to be almost omnipresent? Because he was a master of his time.

Pa Nanagah organized his life in such a way that he had time to do anything that he pleased. This was one key secret of his wealth. He created time for God, time for personal growth, time for family, time for community, time for work, and time for play. When you are not a master of your own time, then your job title and money do not matter – you are poor. When you are a master of your own time, then you are already rich, because you can use that time to build into your life all the other eleven qualities that make up the Success Code.

Positive Social Impact

You come to the place where you realize that the real reason why you have been investing in yourself and making the most of yourself is so that you can have something to give to the world. When you mature on the journey of personal transformation, you become aware that your life is not about you, but about the people that you touch. Making a positive difference in every environment you find yourself becomes not just an obligation but a way of life. It is just who you are. You leave happiness, joy, peace, love, goodness, and progress where ever you go the way a rose casts off its fragrance. Whenever the word "leader" is mentioned we instinctively think of people like Gandhi, King, and Mandela. What we need to realize is that these people are personifications of that spirit within us that calls us to be the change we want to see in every environment we are a part of.

The testimonies in chapter two of this book are only a snapshot of the kinds of things you will hear about the great man Pa Nangah. Imagine that 28 years after his death, a young person reads just a short story about him and exclaims "his story should be taught in schools". What more can you say about how influential his life was? In fact, if a man so moved the world that he continues to inspire greatness in others even in his grave, then such a man is called Nangah.

A young entrepreneur who has founded a construction company said that he is modeling his company after the virtues of Pa Nangah so that one day he should own a company that has the kind of reputation that Nangah Construction Company had. A former student of mine after reading about Pa Nangah said she wished I had taught her lessons such as those portrayed by Pa Nangah's legacy, rather than Immunology. You see? This generation is waking up for the spell that colonial conditioning had cast upon Africans in the name of education. The story of Pa Nangah is igniting a new awakening.

Self-fulfillment Perpetual Growth

I am a firm adherent to the notion that joy is the true measure of success. Genuine joy cannot be faked - it is not some superficial happiness induced by positive thinking techniques. Truly successful people are those who have so balanced their lives that they live permanently it that place which for lack of a better word we usually refer to as bliss, or peace of mind. When you are living in bliss, you are a successful person. The magic of bliss is that it puts you in tune with the flow of life as it evolves and expands. This is how joy and growth are intertwined.

Life is never finished. The universe is a perpetually expanding space and life is a perpetually unfolding mystery. We see it around us every day that the fiction of yesterday is the fact of today, the miracle of yesterday is the standard of today, and the extraordinary accomplishment of yesterday is the routine of today. Life is continually advancing. The final frontier of success, therefore, is not some destination you want to arrive at, some trophy you want to win, some score you want to settle, etc. It is not a person, place, or thing; it is a state. The final frontier of success is to position yourself in the state of mind where you are always working to improve yourself, expand your horizons, and open up to new possibilities.

Pa Nangah had a mastery of the law of joy and increase. He knew that the only way to truly live is to live in harmony with the law of growth. His first giant step was his audacious upgrade from an office clerk to a contractor. When he saw that building houses was his real calling, he created the Nangah Construction Company. He had no intention of just being a self-employed man with enough bread on his table. After each successful project, he set a higher standard for himself and challenged his team to give the world the best building, bridge, or road, ever made in that environment in those days. He had a reputation for demolishing walls that were not straight. He trained his eyes to be sharper than measuring tapes and spirit levels, reason why he could stand at a distance and challenge a measurement that his engineers had made with standard instruments. He created a company to respond to any need that moved him in West Cameroon. This is how he created the brewery company NOBRA, the Bamenda Modern Bakery, Sky Line Hotel, the Nangah Produce Company, the Postal Service, and many others.

If you can imagine yourself entering Pa Nangah's brain and trying to figure out his thought pattern, then one thing you will surely find is that every year, his birthday cake was some great business achievement he had added to his portfolio. Inertia did not know him, stagnation did not exist for him, contentment was not in his dictionary. He celebrated his accomplishments and was grateful for all his blessings, but he also knew that every new achievement was evidence of what was possible. Since he lived for the world and not for himself, he kept imagining bigger dreams and kept achieving them till he died. If he was a soldier in the army, we would have said he died in active duty.

Gratitude was the one most prominent evidence that Pa Nangah was a joyful man. Although his palace was gigantic, fenced, and frightful from a distance, the gates were always thrown wide open on occasions like Christmas and New Year for the whole village to come and feast. He gave without measure, helped his collaborators to create their own businesses, educated the children of strangers even more than some of his own, and stepped out of his car to greet and chat with young people working in his yard.

BECOME IT, THEN YOU WILL SEE IT

When you were a baby, you were fully human because your human DNA was intact. When you were a teenager, you were fully human because your human DNA was intact. When you became an adult, you were still fully human because your human DNA was intact. It is the same human genetic code unfolding your existence along the growth curve from a baby, toddler, infant, teenager, adult, and old age. The success code acts in the same way. When you weave the twelve attributes of the success code into your life, then you have become a successful person. Right now you can be homeless but you are already a successful person. This is the magic of this new philosophy that I have been blessed to channel to the world. Success is about who you are, not what you have.

When you recreate your life after the pattern of the success code, what happens is that day by day, the law of increase will be raising your existence to systematically expanding degrees of experience. Your spiritual awareness will be expanding, your knowledge will be increasing, you will grow into a greater experience of joy, your relationships will become better, you will become healthier, you will start finding avenues for expressing your authentic self, you will start seeing opportunities for building and sustaining a great career, money will start flowing in consistently in ever increasing measure, you will experience a renewed sense of attunement with nature, your influence on the people around you will start becoming visible, and you will go to bed each night grateful that today was better than yesterday and eager for an even better tomorrow. Building the success code into your system is what transforms you into a successful person. The rest is just the gradual unfolding of that success in ever increasing measure.

CHAPTER 5

SAY GOODBYE TO YOUR EXCUSES

Illusions are created to keep human beings drowned in distraction and waste their life force away. A weak and dependent humanity is the perfect prey to the few who are aware of the truth and are using this power to manipulate the masses to feed their greed. The world as we know it is a hallucination, a waking dream in which our only focus is the dollar hunt because everything has been wired to put us in a constant state of fear – the fear of not having money.

All that is needed to free ourselves from this hallucination is to awaken. All that is needed to topple the current socio-economic system is for us to build a critical mass of awakened souls. Several myths have been constructed and fed into our subconscious to make the money illusion seem real. You can call me a master of these myths because they are the myths in which I was raised, and that were responsible for my attaining the height of my career life at the age of 36 while still soaked in financial difficulty. You can do everything else in your life perfectly well, and attain any height you dream of, but until you unveil and debunk the myths about money that have been ingrained in your subconscious mind, you will keep wondering whether there is a hole in your pocket.

The list is far from being exhaustive. I have highlighted these 16 myths based on my experience. Depending on your personal experience and where/how you were raised you may have some myths to add to the list. But I know you will identify with most of these ones. The essence of this exercise is like what happens in a dream. When you are facing grave danger and there is no escape, you suddenly remember that it is just a dream. By remembering, you wake up. When you wake up, you heave a sigh of relief that it was just a dream. It is the same thing with subconscious beliefs, myths, or conditionings. They cast us into a spell and we live our lives in a waking dream controlled by them. When the light of truth shines upon our consciousness and we discover that these beliefs are false, they lose their power and we are free to replace them with the truth.

Myth number 1: Money is real.

Physical money is an illusion. It is not actual money. It is virtual money. The banknote in your pocket is just a piece of decorated paper with a serial number. The reason why you can use that bank note to purchase three apples is because the fiscal community to which you belong has collectively agreed that instead of carrying three apples around, you should carry that piece of paper, which when you give anyone, he/she will recognize it as a legal tender for three apples or any other equivalent commodity.

The value of your currency and how much of it is printed and put in circulation is decided by somebody's signature. There is no other rule. If your central bank prints more money, then you get more of it in your pocket. If they print less, then you have less of it in your pocket. How many units of your currency you can exchange for how many units of a foreign currency depends on how powerful your government is in relation to that other country. If the basic laws of demand, supply, inflation, and deflation, were as we were taught in school, how come prices are instead going up while productivity is increasing? How do you explain the fact that African countries that are endowed with unspeakable deposits of gold, silver, diamonds, copper, iron, oil, and timber will trade 600 units of their currency for 1 unit of the currency of the European countries that feed off them?

If currency was real money, then each country will be as rich as its natural resources. But money is a hoax, created to distract humans while its creators play their game of control and manipulation. Basically, humans are like school children and money is like sweets. A big guy comes along, opens a pack of sweets and spreads it in the air, and while the kids get into a commotion, each one fighting to catch one or two, the big guy is busy doing what he came to do.

Myth number 2: There is separation between you and money.

The illusion that money is a physical object that exists out there, and which can only come to you after you have worked hard for it, contains within it the implication that you and money are two separate realities. The principles formulated by Isaac Newton 300 years ago have served as the basis of modern science. Some of the basic assumptions of science are that reality is solid matter made up of atoms; that the universe is a random assembly of many separate parts; and that the space between the parts is empty. Since the language of science is at the heart of the modern empire we call capitalism, every system is basically an application of these assumptions.

Money is not left out of this flawed premise. It is viewed as a material object that is separate from you, another material being, and you need to perform a combination of physical actions in order to close the gap between you and the money you want. Interestingly, physicists have shocked themselves and the rest of the scientific community with discoveries that are bound to devastate the very core of this 300-year-old civilization. It is now proven beyond reasonable doubt that the building blocks of matter are not atoms, but sub-atomic pockets of light called photons. Beyond the photons, the existence of the Higgs Boson nicknamed the God-particle was recently demonstrated in 2012, thereby proving the existence of the Higgs field. Now, the discovery of the Higgs field is the one discovery that the average materialist scientist would have wished to not happen in his lifetime. Its properties provide material proof that the universe is one pulsating and continuous energy field that gives rise to the multiplicity of forms.

These forms arise from this field, exist within this field, are linked by this field, and return to this field after their transient experience. The field has no beginning and no end, cannot be created or destroyed, is uniformly present on all points of the universe, and certainly exists outside of time and space. This is physics, not some spiritual hocus-pocus, or theology. It, however, bears striking resemblance to the truths that the spiritual traditions and ancient philosophers have always taught about the universe.

With the above in mind, we could say that science is fulfilling its divine destiny, that of providing tangible evidence to things that we have previously accepted on belief alone. What is the implication for you? If the universe is one ocean of energy and every material reality is merely a wave that rises and falls within that ocean in which everything is entangled with everything else, what that means is that the thing called money and you are one. Your separation from it is only in your imagination, and your need to "work" for it is the logical outcome of that false belief.

Myth number 3: Money is scarce.

There is nothing scarce about money. The central bank can print as much paper as it wants. If paper and ink were scarce, then we would have understood why money should be scarce. If money was backed up by gold reserves as it used to be, then we could have understood why there should be more money in some countries and less of it in some countries. The amount of paper in circulation, in the name of money, simply depends on how much of it the people call it forth, through the creation of value.

The more value you create in the economy, the more the central bank is forced to print money to serve as the means by which that value circulates in the economy. It is that simple. This is a system that anyone in the world can take advantage of. Since currency is virtual money, you can also develop virtual solutions to shift the tides of money in your favor. Money is no longer backed by gold. It is backed by ideas that create value. More money can be mined from the human brain than has ever been mined from the oil fields of the world. The technology revolution has proven it. While western governments are perpetuating wars and political unrest in endowed countries so as to steal oil and other resources, the boys and girls of Silicon Valley are busy becoming billionaires without breaking a sweat.

Of course, these are truths that the rich people are hoping that the average person should never know or take advantage of. Imagine for a second that the headquarters of Microsoft, Apple, Google, and Facebook were to be moved to Bamenda Cameroon. The value shift will be so massive that this town will become like San Francisco overnight. So, what would have caused the change? Not extra gold growing on the hills of Mbatu, but the value movement. I hope every youth in every so-called developing country gets this clue. No colonial power needs to give you economic freedom. No government needs to change in order for you to get out of poverty. If you discover that money is a hoax, and focus on creating value, you will turn the money tables.

Myth number 4: Money is the root of evil.

Money is evil, yet you need money to buy flowers for your girlfriend. Money is evil, yet you need money to pay for your studies. Money is evil, yet you need money to pay for your housing, clothing, feeding, transportation, communication, healthcare, and so on. Money is evil, yet you need money to buy the Bible you call the word of God. Money is evil, yet your church always wants more of it. There is something dumb about this kind of logic, don't you think?

When the subject of money comes up, many people are quick to refer you to the Bible saying, "money is the root of all evil". That is the consequence of not reading the bible for yourself. This saying is a twisted version of Paul's first letter to Timothy, Chapter 6 and verse 10, which reads, "For the love of money is the root of all evil: which while some coveted after, they have erred from the faith, and pierced themselves through with many sorrows." It is clear from this text itself that it is not money that is the root of evil, but the love of money. And the word love here does not mean "affinity" but "lust". The second part of the verse makes it clear that the root of evil is the erring from faith, as a result of coveting or lusting after money.

Hypnotizing you with religious language to subconsciously reject money as evil, is an excellent scheme to make you not be interested in money so that you can happily work for those who have use for it. So, while you are laboring and starving on earth in expectation of your reward in heaven, your priests, pastors, and prophets are enjoying their own reward here on earth, wearing the clothes you should be wearing, driving the cars you should be driving, living in the homes you should be living in and flying in the jets you should be flying in.

Myth number 5: Having much money means you are bad.

The idea that money is scarce means that there is not enough money to go around, for everybody to have a comfortable amount. In this line of thought, it is therefore immoral to want much money, because to have more means depriving someone else of their share. Do you really believe that? I see money as the symbol of freedom. If you are a bad person, money will give you the opportunity to do more bad things. If you are a good person, more money will give you the opportunity to do more good things.

When I visit an orphanage and donate a bag of food or money for school fees for a child, the joy I see in those children's eyes make me give thanks to God for having provided me with the money to perform that act of kindness. If you want to see how much love is locked up inside a dollar bill, find a homeless man under a bridge on a winter night and give him a dollar to buy a plate of hot soup. The pieces of paper are not money. It does not matter how much of them you have in the bank or in your ceiling. People can only have as much money as the value that passes through them, so that amount of money you have has nothing to do with the amount of money someone else has. And there is nothing moral or immoral about it.

If you own a company that employs hundreds of people and your product or service makes life easier and better for millions of people, you will naturally be a millionaire, whether you are a good husband or not, whether you go to church or not. If you are the most pious member of your church but your value chain is limited to driving your pastor around, you will be broke. Yes, your place may be secure in heaven, but in this world of Caesar, you will be deprived of every comfort money can buy. And if being broke leads your kids into crime and drugs because they are out of school and their mom has left you, you had better not blame God or the devil for your predicament.

I can assure you that spending money feels better than justifying why you don't or should not have money. "Blessed are the poor" is a lie. What the Beatitude says is that "Blessed are the poor in spirit". Mind you that having money does not necessarily mean that you are rich in spirit and not having money does not necessarily mean that you are poor in spirit. If you look down on your neighbor because you have money and he doesn't, you are rich in spirit. Conversely, if you envy or hate your uncle or are always talking about him because he has money and you don't, you are rich in spirit.

To not have cash and be spiritually poor means that you had the chance to get rich, but out of your own free will, you chose not to, because you freely and willingly renounced earthly comforts and pleasures in favor of spiritual pursuits. I wonder how many such people exist or can exist in this capitalistic world in which the only thing left for us to package and sell is oxygen (apart from the one in the intensive care unit). Most poor people simply use religious rationalizations as a means of cushioning their conscience. If you want 100 reasons why it is good to stay poor, go and ask my dad. If you want 100 reasons why it is good to get rich, go and ask my uncle. If you find a priest or pastor who can give you 10 reasons why you should not give money to his church, bring him let us transfer the keys of heaven to him.

There is nothing blessed about poverty. And there is nothing evil about riches. If your childhood was in any way similar to mine, you will know that life is a little more fun when there are a few banknotes in your wallet.

Myth number 6: To get money you must work hard.

Humans are born to work. But there is a world of difference between labor and creative self-expression. Labor is when I have to trade my time and muscle for a loaf of bread, and most of the times it doesn't matter whether I like what I am doing or not, because it is about paying the bills. This is what most of our jobs are really about, right? Creative self-expression is when you are doing the work that is in harmony with your passion. The work serves as a spontaneous outlet for your specialized knowledge and skills, unique gifts and talents, and as you do it you feel fulfilled and expanded.

We have been sold the lie that we must labor in order to get money, and when we need more money, we must labor harder. The truth is, the more you labor, the more you waste your life force and the poorer you get as a result. True wealth is effortless. It comes as a natural response to those who are living their authentic lives, through creative self-expression.

Myth number 7: To get plenty of money you must compete.

Any environment that is built on the assumption of scarcity must have competition as the foundation paradigm for human interaction. The desire to survive is inherent in everyone. If we all must survive but there is not enough to go round for everyone, then survival of the fittest becomes the rule. Beyond survival, we have comfort. Wanting plenty of money means that you have transcended the basic needs, have gone beyond survival, and now want to be comfortable.

When we are programmed to believe that money is scarce and that we must struggle to rid someone of theirs in order to have more, we fall into the mindset that says in order to have more we must compete more. In this mindset, we see other people, other businesses, other ventures as competitors rather than collaborators. We treat others as enemies because we assume that we and they are after the same trophy and the only way for us to have that trophy is to stop them from having it. This is a terrible lie. There is more money in creativity than in competition. There is more business in innovation than in competition.

Myth number 8: To get rich you must get your hands dirty.

There is financial freedom, which is basically freedom from the slavery of want, debt, and all other financial worries. There is having plenty of money, which is really a matter of being financially free enough to live an expanded life beyond mere survival. Then there is being rich, which is the stage at which you are literally swimming in money. Those who have business empires that cover the whole world, spend as much time on private jets as you spend on taxis and subways, and give more money to charity than the annual budget of some developing countries; these are the really rich guys.

In a world where it is considered normal for an ordinary guy to be worth 80 billion dollars, I personally think it is a lot harder to make excuses for why you chose poverty than to just focus on getting rich yourself. Now, one of the psychological drugs with which people sedate themselves is this idea that you cannot get rich without getting your hands dirty. The general idea is that for you to be rich and stay rich you must belong to a blood-drinking cult, be a drug lord, a weapons dealer, or all such things. While it is true that dirty fellows do lots of dirty stuff and get lots of dirty money, it is also true that clean fellows do lots of clean stuff and get lots of clean money. Again, the problem is not with the money but with you. Money is just energy, and energy always takes the form you give to it.

Myth number 9: Money depends on your biology.

We have been fed lies, such as there is a chosen race that God blessed thousands of years ago through their ancestors, such that whatever they do, prospers. We have heard conspiracy theories about certain families that are in control of all the money in the world, and wealth, power, and success only flow in their bloodlines. While the Jews know themselves as God's chosen people, my Mbatu people also know themselves as God's chosen people. In fact, the belief in a special divine calling and relationship is at the root of every religion.

It is now just a matter of who had the historical advantage of selling his own idea of God and consequently imposing his own culture on the rest of us. And we know that it is thanks to the ancient Roman Empire that the so-called western world is predominantly Christian. I find it puzzling that there are people today who call themselves Christians but still speak of 'God's chosen people' in biological terms.

Then we come to the issue of families. If your great-grandfather was the inventor of Coca-Cola or Heineken, for example, and did a great job at building a family tradition that sustained and grew the wealth, is it not just a matter of common sense that you, the great-grandson should be a CEO at 25years old if you are following the family work ethic? If your ancestors invented the idea of lending silver coins for interest, and eventually perfected the idea of banking, and then the governments that were cropping up, enlisted the aid of these money experts, is it not a matter of common sense that the central banks, regional banks, international monetary fund, and all other such *njangui* houses can be traced back to these families? If you were a descendant of such a family, will you be rich because your DNA is made up of Euros and Dollars rather than base-pairs, or will you be rich because of the natural law of evolution and compound interest?

A little investigation will prove to you that 99% of today's millionaires and billionaires are first generation wealthy people. In other words, they came from parents that were broke and built their wealth by themselves. On the other hand, experience has shown that leaving a fortune in the hands of children that are not sufficiently trained to manage it will ultimately ruin them. There is nothing biological about wealth. You can get rich if you want to, and are ready to do what your father did not do.

Myth number 10: Money comes to you as a result of belonging to certain secret societies.

The saying that "birds of a feather flock together" seems to be at the root of this suspicion. Rich people make friends with rich people and poor people make friends with poor people. When rich people are together, they discuss money and opportunity. When poor people are together, they discuss rich people. Looking for mysterious clouds to cast over rich people is a subconscious strategy poor people always use to console themselves in their failure to get rich. The worse part of this is that they teach it to their children, so the children grow up knowing that they won't get out of poverty because the only means available is to join a cult that does bad things to other people, and they are not willing to do that.

I have no argument against the existence of cults, but I certainly have an argument against the idea that the only way to get rich is to join a cult. If you look at things on a deeper level, you will realize that cults are basically spiritual institutions like churches that have an organized system of manipulating the subconscious minds of their members to awaken their powers and direct them toward the attainment of their individual and collective goals. Secret societies are therefore for people who are too weak to do stuff on their own. Those who are rich and selfish also enjoy the idea of being gods over the rest of the people. One way of keeping other people from getting rich is by hiding from them the secret to their wealth. The secret is ridiculously simple. What is complicated to dismantle are the mental barriers that have been built around this secret for centuries by those who did not want you to find it. When you awaken, you will find that this secret is You.

Myth number 11: Money comes to you as a result of following certain religious systems.

If you do a census of rich people in the world, you will notice that they are a fair representation of the religions of the world. If you zone in on one religion, say Christianity, you will notice that rich Christians are a fair representation of the various Christian denominations. If you pick rich Catholics, you will find still that among them there are those who cannot remember the last time they went for confession or paid their church contributions. In every church, there are rich and poor folks.

If there was a report card on which Christians were ranked annually based on number of church services or masses attended, number of times they cleaned the church, how often they helped their priests and pastors with laundry, how frequently they prayed novenas, how often they went for pilgrimages, how regular they were with their tithes and offerings, how often they received the sacraments, and so on, poor people will always top the class. If money was a special blessing from God for being churchy, then I know quite a number of people who would be swimming in money today, including myself. In fact, Africa would be more developed than America.

Many are those who happily cheer up their pastors as they preach to them that "the wealth of the "wicket" is laid up for the righteous". They are no longer eager for the rapture. They are now eager for the mysterious hand of God that will shake up the economy so that the money that the "wicket" ones are amassing will come to them the Christians. If you care you can go ahead confessing that the worldly or so-called unrighteous people are working for you, while the same pastor who is keeping you in that state of hallucination is collecting an offering to buy his next car or private jet.

Myth number 12: Money comes to you as a result of being in a particular geographical environment.

There are rich people in Angola and there are rich people in Canada. There are wealthy people in Australia and there are wealthy people in Mexico. Experience itself is proof that wealth is never a matter of location. It happens every day, everywhere that two people who started the same business with the same capital in the same location on the same day wind up some years later totally different. One has grown into a business empire while the other remains on the same spot.

In the Cameroonian grass field area, a *njangui* is a mutual financial aid group constituted by a small trust-based community, in which people pool little savings together periodically, and members take turns to receive the pooled capital and use for their individual needs. Alternatively, the pooled capital can serve as a reservoir for collateral-free micro-credit to members at interest rates fixed by the members themselves. This practice can be found across almost the whole of Sub-Saharan Africa.

I recently came across an interesting story that said that there is one such *njangui* groups operated by a group of South African women, which rotates the same capital that one of the major South African banks started with some years ago. Your *njangui* group is a bank, but you don't know it; you make better hamburgers than McDonald's, but you don't know it; your natural palm wine is of greater value than imported Spanish red wine, but you don't know it. If geography has anything to do with wealth creation, it can only be so if your movement to a certain place has had an impact on your brain. Rest assured that there in New York, the financial capital of planet earth, the number of poor, hungry, sick, and homeless people is greater than the total population of some countries in Africa.

Myth number 13: You must be of a certain age before you can have money.

The saying that "age is wisdom" used to be true in the age in which apprenticeship was the only means of education, and experience was the only measure of financial earning power. The new age is being pioneered by kids like Mark Zuckerberg, co-founder of Facebook, who at 33 years of age is not only a billionaire but is ranked by Forbes Magazine as the fifth richest man in the world in 2017. If age was money, then I should be a few billions richer than Mark and my dad's wealth should be almost three times greater than mine. But that is not the case.

The old folks have a hard time accepting that while in their days you needed to work your ass out to retire with a few thousands of dollars in the bank and be respected in your community as a rich guy, today, kids become millionaires even before they had had time to complete their degree and gotten married. I look forward to the day kids will celebrate their 18th birthdays as millionaires, so that we as a society should stop making the money chase the priority of life, and reorganize our lives around the values of compassion, sharing, and togetherness that we once knew.

Myth number 14: You must have a certain education before you can have money.

I started learning my lesson when I was a fourth-year medical laboratory science student at the University of Buea. As part of my graduation requirements, I had to spend a year of clinical laboratory rotations in the teaching hospitals in Yaoundé. Guess who provided me shelter the first week I entered Yaoundé? My childhood friend Caleb, who had gotten bored with the school routine and dropped out of secondary school to go and learn the furniture trade. I have so many rich friends and relations without certificates that it often makes me wonder whether all the time I spent in school was really worth it.

By the time he died in 1990, Pa Daniel Nangah was the wealthiest person in the English-speaking part of Cameroon. He was probably the wealthiest Cameroonian civilian because those who are the wealthiest today have grown most of their wealth only in recent years. In fact, as you must have noticed from the testimonies in Chapter 2 of this book, during the late 1970s and early 1980s, he appeared in the Cameroon Year Book as Cameroon's richest man. Buildings that were erected by his construction company still appear more modern and durable than those constructed by engineers of today. He built not only a palace for himself, but also a church, school, and health center, roads, and bridges for his community. He owned shares in almost every multinational company in the country and sat on the boards of many. He owned property in Europe and America and sent many brilliant youths who came across his path for studies abroad.

There are many intellectuals and millionaires today who are the fruit of Nangah's largess, even though they were not his biological children and neither they nor their parents had anything to give Nangah in return. He employed Italian architects to work for him and he paid them as expatriates. He lived where he wished, drove the luxury car he wished, even married which woman he wished. Till date the government still owes him balance from government contracts, and what has happened to his assets, shares, and stocks is beyond my finding out.

My point is that by my family standards, this uncle of mine was uneducated. In that same family we have academic professors, accountants, PhDs, teachers, administrators, engineers, doctors, and lawyers, but the uneducated uncle, who left this earth twenty-seven years ago, is still the wealthiest member of our family, our village, and our town. I enjoy the bliss of knowledge, the glory of the academic gown especially when you are a dean or rector, and the beauty of the awards and certificates. But I know that none of that has anything to do with money. Trust me, I have seen both sides of the coin.

Myth number 15: Only certain trades or professions can get you rich.

I don't know any doctor, engineer or lawyer that is richer than Mayweather, Jay-Z, Ronaldo, or Serena. But where I grew up, if you said that you wanted to grow up and become an athlete or musician, your parents would beat the hell out of you or take you to the village doctor. Children dream of their future based on their passion, but as they go through school, we condition them to start thinking within the box of what society considers fashionable white-collar careers.

Eventually, they get into the rote routine of memorizing the classroom knowledge, making the good grades, passing the standardized tests, getting the scholarships, and graduating from the ivy league universities. Environmental conditioning through parents, peers, churches, media, and a controlled educational system end up fossilizing human genius. By the time we become adults we are robots that have been fine-tuned to be excellent at a particular job or trade, in exchange for a fixed wage that is never enough to pay the ever-increasing bills and debts. If you look around you and try to profile those who are living in financial prosperity, you will notice that they come from all walks of life. There are rich doctors and poor doctors, rich pastors and poor pastors, rich carpenters and poor carpenters, rich hairdressers and poor hairdressers, rich thieves and poor thieves.

Myth number 16: There is a secret to getting rich.

This is probably the greatest hoax ever constructed and by far the most successful in keeping human beings in bondage. By buying the lie that there is a secret to money, the world has distracted you from what you should have been thinking and doing in this moment (the only place where life really exists) and placed your mind in the wonderland of the eternal seeker. You are forever seeking the secret and never finding it because by seeking it outside yourself, you are guaranteed to not look in the only place where you should be looking. If at all there is a secret, then you will wake up one day to find that the secret is you.

The secret has been you, all along. And so, the only problem with your life is that you left your home where your true power is, and went out in search for a power outside of yourself, which does not exist. You are a wealthy being, by virtue of who you are. When your energy is focused on your true identity and your life is the channeling of your authentic self, money will flow in your life as naturally as leaves grow on a tree.

The power to excel in life is not found in books, sermons, churches, seminars, secret societies, or any anointed hand. The kingdom of heaven is within you, therefore, the secret of success is within you. Any teacher who asks you to look here or go there is a con. A true prophet is the one who shows you how to look within.

CHAPTER 6

HOW TO CREATE THE SUCCESS YOU DESIRE

If you grew up in the village and spent your childhood helping your mother on the farm, this will come as a surprise to you. Yes, it is surprising that the greatest wisdom in the universe has been locked up in your body unused for all these years. You have been fooled into treasuring the classroom lectures and the school certificates, and you have failed to realize that there is no amphitheater, no professor, no textbook, that can teach you anything more valuable than the education that was systematically programmed into your cells by nature itself. My mother, Manwing Regina Kieng, who never had as much as a Primary school report card, remains the most revered professor in my life, and I am about to show you why. God reveals Himself in strange ways, and "The 12 Fundamental Laws of Success", which I learned through my interaction with my mother on the farm, is clearly one of those strange ways.

Let us examine how nature reveals its secrets through the farm, and how our life is just like the farm.

Law #1: A Solid Foundation

Every village woman has her farm that she identifies with as the source of livelihood for her household. She has her farming tools and farm basket with which she interacts with her farm. She has a lifestyle that boils down to a predictable relationship with her farm. Every life needs to be solidly grounded in a sense of identity and purpose. Every person is supposed to be actively pursuing their purpose through a specific career. Success is supposed to be a lifestyle.

Law #2: Deliberate Creation

Different types of crops do well on different types of soils. So, you know where to plant yams, where to plant corn, and where to plant vegetables. It is the same with your life. Your health, your career, your relationships, your finances, etc., all combine to make up a successful life but each one must be nurtured in a unique way. For each area of your life to flourish, you need to consciously identify the need, intentionally choose the change, then cultivate the specific combination of specialized knowledge, skills, and attitudes that are unique to that domain. Success does not just happen; it is the result of deliberate creation.

Law #3: Rhythm

There is a season to saw and a season to reap. If you do not sow during the planting season, you will wind up as a beggar or at best spend a lot of money on what others are enjoying for free. There is a time to work and a time to enjoy; there is a time to invest and a time to reap the profits. Your youth is the planting season of your life and your adulthood is the harvesting season. You will enjoy in later life if only you sowed in your youth. If you waste the sowing season trying to use shortcuts to reap fruits that are meant for a different season, it will not be long before you will find yourself bankrupt in both material and immaterial things.

Law #4: Preparation

Before sowing, you must clear the bush, till the soil, and prepare the ground. Same thing in real life. You cannot think, talk, pray, and wait for miracles. You must get your hands dirty, sweat it out, and do some work. Prayer is for revelation, but actualization takes work. You must cleanse your mind of the limiting stereotypes that have been programmed into you by society; you must cultivate the specialized knowledge and skills needed to succeed, then you must get busy.

Law #5: Correspondence

The quality of the seed you sow determines the quality of harvest you get. So, common sense demands that you select the very best seeds. Also, the specific seed you sow determines the specific crop you harvest. It is impossible to plant yams and harvest potatoes. In life, your audacious goals and your commitment to excellence represent the good seeds. Small goals stimulate mediocre effort and mediocre effort engenders mediocre results. Mighty goals inspire massive inspired action, and massive inspired action engenders excellent results. The law of identical harvest can never be broken.

Law #6: Growth

After preparing the best soil and sowing the best seed, you wait on the law of growth to do its part. You do not dig up the seed every morning to see what is happening to it. You trust in that power that is greater than you to convert your seed into a harvest because it must be so by the law of creation. It has nothing to do with what you think or say or believe. The law must fulfill itself. In real life, this is the aspect called faith. But people don't realize that faith simply means allowing the law of the universe to fulfill itself through the seeds you have sown. This is scientific faith.

Law #7: Persistence

When you sow corn, you wait for it to mature in its due season. You do not get restless and uproot it and plant beans or something else. Do you? When you set an objective in life and start a project to achieve it, you have to persist until you achieve it. Changing your mind every day and chasing something new every day without having achieved the previous one is the perfect recipe for failure. Learn to pray without ceasing, till you get what you have asked for.

Law #8: Passion

While the crop is growing you visit it regularly to weed the grass, munch the soil, and keep animals away, and sometimes add fertilizer. In life you must protect your dreams from the birds of peoples negative thinking and discouragement, you must weed off any people in your life who are trying to run you down rather than build you up. You must keep feeding your mind and building your faith with inspiration. You must be a life-long learner who is always improving and becoming more fertile. You must surround yourself with people who have done what you are doing so that their energy and guidance can serve as manure for your dream. Your passion is your fuel. Only those who are in love with their dream see their dream come true.

Law #9: Networking

Sometimes you team up with other people to form a farming njangui. The whole team lands on your farm and brings down the whole hill on one day. The following day they move to the other person's farm. Every member of the group is a specialist at something. Because of the massive action and division of labor, work is lighter and enjoyable, and everyone ends up with more work done than he or she could possibly have done alone. This is the power of the mastermind alliance. You need to build your personal success network using people whose hearts and minds resonate with yours. This is what Jesus meant when he said that "when two or three are gathered in my name I am in their midst". Psychology has proven that when two or more minds are focused on a single objective, there is a resultant mind that is more powerful than the sum of its parts.

Law #10: Receiving

When it is harvesting time, you do not ask for any one's permission or approval in order to enjoy the fruits of your labor. You do not beg God for a miracle or doubt if you deserve the fruits. No, all that nature has poured out as harvest through your farm, is automatically yours. When you are harvesting the fruits of your labor, you do not make apologies to those who envy you or claim you had some advantages that they didn't. You do not feel guilty that you have a rich harvest and some people don't. No, you reap with joy and you don't leave some food behind. When success comes to you it comes in a measure that can be overwhelming and cause you to wonder if you actually deserve it. Remember that it is not a random blessing but the fulfillment of the law. They are the seeds you cultivated that have multiplied. It is not a miracle, it is perfectly natural.

There are people who will say you are successful because you have joined a cult, or because you come from a rich home or because you are well connected. Some of your friends will try to make you feel guilty for being so successful while they are not. Nonsense! Enjoy your success. The only thing they can do to help themselves is to let your example inspire them. If they fail to do so, it is not your fault.

Law #11: Multiplication

The first thing you do with any harvest is that you select the very best crop and save it as a seed for the next season. No matter what form of success you enjoy, always save the best as a seed for your greater success. For example, open a bank account into which you save 10% of every money that enters your hand and make sure you never withdraw from it. The day will come when you will need capital for your next project, then you will repeat the cycle. This is what the law of tithing is really about. Harvest the first tenth of every gift you receive and save it as seed. A tenth of your time, your energy, your money, your relationships, your talent, everything, should be invested into the creation of the better version of your tomorrow.

Law #12: Giving

As you enjoy your harvest, you find that it tastes sweeter when shared; the power of sharing, the meaning of community or communion. Sharing your good fortune with others and bringing joy to their lives is the ultimate success. No matter how many hours we spend each day in worship and adoration, sharing with others is the most powerful form of worship, for it testifies in a tangible way that we recognize the presence of God in others. No matter how thankful we say we are, giving is the only tangible proof that we are grateful to our Source because by giving, we become the source to others.

***

Here I have given you a resumé of the Twelve Fundamental Laws of Success. No matter which book you read, which seminar you attend, which courses you take, which movies you watch on the subject of life, everything they teach you will always boil down to these twelve laws. On very rare occasions will you find them articulated in the comprehensive manner in which we have done them here.

Yes, by returning to the lowliest of places (our mothers' farms), we have unveiled a model of life that beats all the knowledge of the world. This wisdom has been lying fallow within you because you have not been aware that it was there. You were busy chasing for knowledge in the amphitheaters and seeking success secrets in books. Now that I have caused you to remember what you know, wake up now and put it to use to transform your life and your world.

CHAPTER 7

BUILD YOUR WEALTH CREATION SYSTEM

I strongly believe that money is as vital to human success as fuel is vital to the smooth functioning of a vehicle. This is why I have dedicated the final chapter of this book to the subject of building your own wealth creation system. The problem with earning money is that the amount you can earn is always limited by the number of hours you can work in a week. People who are really rich are those who know how to *make* money. So how about learning how you too can *make* money? Perhaps you don't want to be a billionaire. Perhaps you don't want to be a millionaire.

Perhaps you just want to make enough money to live a comfortable life, say $100,000 a year if you are in the USA or 6million FCFA a year if you are in Cameroon. How can you make this money without slaving for several hours a day, six days a week, all week, all year? How can you make this money and still have time to spend it? How can you make this money and still have the freedom to do the work you enjoy doing, be with the people you love being with, go to the places that thrill you, and do the things that give you an expanded experience of life? This is only possible if you are making money not from your efforts but from systems you have built.

A system is basically a set of connected things or parts that form a complex whole. What are the things that generate money? We have specialized knowledge, skill, labor, commodities, services, assets, institutions, time, and markets.

Knowledge

Those who have specialized knowledge offer this knowledge in exchange for money. Consultancy, writing, etc., is basically the packaging and selling of knowledge.

Labor

People exchange their physical effort for money. Labor requires your physical presence at the place of work. It is your body that gets things done.

Skill

Apart from general labor, there are specialized skills sets that make people professionals in their various domains. There are defined skills sets and attributes that make someone a professional. When you are not a professional, then you can only work as a general laborer.

Commodities

If you have something to sell you get money in return. Raw Commodities are usually cheaper than transformed products. So, the business of transforming raw materials into useful end products is in itself a gold mine.

Services

Services as intangible commodities. People pay for any service that helps people meet their needs for health, security, communication, entertainment, companionship, information, etc.

Assets

An asset is any item of economic value owned by you, that can be converted into cash. Any form of investment that puts money in your pocket is an asset (for example, land, rental house, stocks, bonds, savings, etc.). The opposite of an asset is a liability. Anything you own that takes money out of your pocket is a liability (for example, rents, mortgage, debts, car, credit cards, cable bill, phone and internet subscription, etc.). The net balance between your assets and liabilities determine whether you are rich or poor. If you ensure that for every dollar that goes out, ten dollars come in, then you will get wealthy in no time.

Institutions

Money flows through a chain of institutions from the central bank through commercial banks and businesses to reach your pocket.

Time

Time has a compounding effect on money. It makes assets and debts grow, thereby increasing profit on assets, and interest (debt) on liabilities.

Markets

A market is not a place. It is the available demand for the labor, commodity, or service you have to sell. It is also the combination of economic factors that affect the growth of your assets and the production, packaging, and distribution of your goods and services.

You

You may not realize it, but the most valuable link in the money chain is your individuality. The unique personality traits, experiences, trials, failures, successes, failures, joys, sorrows, and relationships that you have been through constitute a delicate mix that is called you. Why is it that if you place ten people in the kitchen to cook a certain dish with the same recipe, the ten dishes all taste different? Your uniqueness is the most valuable commodity in the market, and if you find a way of leveraging this uniqueness, you will get rich.

A STEP-BY-STEP STRATEGY

To build a personal wealth creation system means to deliberately develop a strategy through which the above factors can come together to make money for you. When you have a system that works, the system will ALWAYS make more money for you than it is possible for you to make from your personal effort alone. And that is why we need systems that make money for us. We have seen that the only way for you to live your authentic life is for you not to have money worries. You won't have money worries if you have a system that is pouring money into your bank account even while you sleep, right?

The good news is that you don't need to have a business degree in order to build a wealth creation system for yourself. Purpose, passion, and common sense make up 99% of what is required. Once you have built your system, you can then hire experts in the various domains to work for you in sustaining and expanding your system. I, who am writing this book have never been to business school. This is not an MBA course that you may be frightened into thinking is not applicable to you. Anyone can do it. All that is needed is a shift in your thinking. Here now is the process:

1. Make an inventory of your abilities, skills, knowledge, talent or natural gifts.

If you start making a list of your personal strengths, unique gifts and talents, and the knowledge, skill, and attributes you have built through your life experiences, you will be amazed to find out how wealthy you really are. There are no two people on earth like you. Your genetic make-up, the circumstances or your birth, your childhood, personal trials, education, spiritual experiences, surroundings, travels, and all that you have been through, have worked together to wire your brain in a way that makes you the only version of you on this planet. What that means is that there is something that only you can create, and there is a way of doing something that is unique to you.

2. Select which of these traits constitutes your super-powers.

Of all your positive traits, what can you say is your superpower? What is that thing that when you start doing, time just ceases to exist? What is that thing that everyone knows you are a genius at? What is that thing that people always compliment you for? What is it that makes you come alive and want to stay in it? It may be one thing, or it may be a combination of two or more things, but what is certain is that there is no being on earth that does not have a super-power.

3. Consider which commodity or service you can develop out of your super-power.

Get to work and figure out how your super-power can be turned into a product or service that serves others. If you are a naturally funny person who cracks jokes spontaneously, how about becoming a stand-up comedian? And if the opportunities for stand-up comedy are limited in your environment, how about setting up an online comedy channel? If people always lick their fingers after eating your food, how come you are still a jobless housewife? Why not open a restaurant? And if opening a restaurant is too demanding because you don't have capital, why not create and market a home delivery brand so that you can work from the comfort of your home? If you are in retirement, isn't it time to chronicle your life in the form of a book that young people can benefit from?

4. Research the market for your commodity or service.

Your market is basically the people that need your product or service. The best products and services are those that meet the felt needs that people have. Many businesses develop products and services they want and then spend fortunes in marketing and advertising to basically 'force' people to buy things they do not need. Smart entrepreneurship begins with knowing what people really need, want, and will not resist buying if it shows up. After people, the next market factor is 'place'. Some years ago, a market meant a geographical area like your school, village, town, or province, or state, or maybe the country.

These days, your market can extend anywhere on earth where there is someone who needs what you have, so long as you figure out a smooth system of payment and delivery. The magic of the internet has made this possible. Then there is the price at which you will sell your product or service. Find out the purchasing power of your customers, find out how much they are willing to pay for your product or service, factor in your production and distribution cost and other running costs like taxes and salaries, then mark up this amount with the profit you intend to make.

5. Create an environment that will help you sharpen and perfect your marketable attributes.

Building a product or service that appeals to thousands or millions of people requires that you stay on top of your game. If you already feel like you are the best at what you do, maybe because it is overtly unique, then you are good to go. Most times, you will need to optimize your preparation by sharpening a few skills here and there. It doesn't necessarily mean going back to school to get an extra degree, but it does imply that you have to become a life-long learner.

Read books that are related to your field, watch videos, attend seminars, take courses, or go and do an apprenticeship at a related business. You may be the best cook in the world but the best restaurants are owned by the best marketers who employ the best cooks. Make an inventory of all the skills you will need for your business, and create a strategy for acquiring these skills as you go along.

6. Set a goal for yourself.

Remember that the reason why you are doing this is so that you can free yourself from your job, cut yourself loose from the money hypnosis, and live your life in freedom. Your goal should be a picture of your ideal life with all the money and time you could ever need. What would your life look like if you had all the money you could ever want and all the time you need to spend it? Put this goal in writing. Make sure your goal is as specific, measurable, realistic, attainable, and time-bound.

There should be a specific amount of money that represents your annual income or your net worth. Your goal should include tangible and recognizable items that will serve as landmarks to help you know you have arrived, such as a certain amount of money in the bank, or a home in a specific neighborhood. A realistic goal simply means something that is within the frame of possibility on this earth. Can a human being do it? Has it ever been done? Your goal is attainable if you can trace a logical sequence between you and the achievement of the goal. It is an answer to the question, "is it possible for you?" Your goal should have a time-frame. It is helpful to have a big life-time goal, then break it down into medium-term goals (5 – 10 years) and short team goals (3 months to one year).

7. Cultivate the faith that this goal will become a reality.

A goal is a picture you have painted. Faith is the power that puts life into the picture and transforms it into a living thing. Keep in mind that the level you are at in life is always the material counterpart of the state of consciousness you are occupying. Hence, for you to move from one level to another, you must raise your consciousness to that level where you want to belong. It is impossible to rise to a new level through physical means.

Unfortunately, this is what humanity has been trying to do for ages. This is what has been taught in schools, churches, business seminars, and motivational books. Willpower, physical effort, and positive thinking can never make you change your level. Your level changes as an outward response to your movement on the scale of consciousness. Saturate your brain (conscious mind) with inspired texts, and reflect on these truths until they dig a trough through your heart (subconscious mind).

When you attain the height of an elevated being, the things you are seeking will begin to feel natural for you. The goal will become so alive that it will begin to pull you toward itself and the physical movements involved in reaching the goal will become easy and fun. All the positive mental attitudes of self-confidence, enthusiasm, optimism, passion, persistence, and all the traits that you find in successful people, are all offshoots of faith. Make it a tradition to read, reflect, apply, reflect, read, reflect, apply, reflect, read again…This is the metaphysical spiral that constantly raises you higher and higher on the physical realm.

8. Build a team that will help you turn your goal into reality.

If your super-power is coding and your goal is to design an e-commerce platform that links farmers with households so that housewives can get fresh foodstuff delivered to them straight from the farm, then you want to focus your time and energy actually designing the software, right? The need for a team becomes immediately evident. You need a marketer on your team to help you figure out how the software will reach the housewives and farmers and make them love it. You need to design the software in a way that resonates with housewives and farmers, and for that, you need advice from actual housewives and farmers. You need someone who will finance your project, and so on. You cannot do things alone. And even if you can manage alone, there is always a limit to how far you can go alone.

Teamwork is magic. Build a team of three or more people who share your dream and are as passionate as you in making it come true. It could be your family members, friends, church members, members of your social group, etc. The key is to have people with the specialized knowledge and skills you need, and who are emotionally connected with you enough to believe in what you are doing.

9. Design and test a prototype for your commodity or service.

A prototype is a sample. Use the resources you have available to produce a sample of your product or service. The first test should be between you and your team. Every artist knows that the painting or the poem or the song is never as perfect as the mental ideal that inspired the art. It is the same with an invention or a product.

You have to produce as many prototypes as possible so that you can satisfy yourself that the one you are choosing as the final product is the best possible option. The next step is to show off your prototype to a carefully selected sample of potential customers and hear what they think about it. Use their feedback to improve your prototype to meet their expectations.

10. Patent your prototype

The idea of intellectual property is almost unknown to people in the developing countries. While you are busy burning the midnight candle to bless the world with a new invention or product, there are predators stalking the market for the next big idea that they can use their money to transform into a big business. If you do not protect your idea by acquiring patent rights for it, then you may have worked in vain.

Someone next door can catch your idea, rename it, mass produce it, and make a big business out of it while you continue to languish at the corner store. If your invention is patented, then you have a chance of receiving offers from investors. Patent your idea from the word go so that you will have the peace of mind to grow your business at the rate you want, till the day you feel like selling it and retiring, or passing it on to your children.

11. Develop a marketing and distribution plan for your business.

What is the mechanism through which your product or service will leave your hands into the hands of your customers? Will you set up a physical distribution network involving physical sales outlets, or will you set up an e-commerce website that you will promote on social media? Your distribution plan should be a unique one that responds to the geographical distribution of your customers and the communication network that links them together. Efficiency is key. Nowadays, if you put together the idea of pick-up points in strategic locations, the power of the internet and social media, and the ease of online or mobile payments, you can come up with a smart marketing and distribution plan for almost any kind of product or service.

12. Launch your business.

One concrete action is always worth more than a thousand well-written plans. Just get started. The advantage of building a business out of what you love is that you have fun doing it and you are not subject to the stress involved with fearing that it might fail. Also, you often build such businesses as an aside to your day job, such that you are not under pressure to start making money from it as fast as possible.

Again, beginning small gives you a guilt-free pass to fail as many times as it takes before you find that winning ticket. Once the basics are in place, start your business. Keep an open ear to the feedback you are receiving and use it to improve on your business. Realize that just as the product itself needed a prototype, your initial marketing strategy could also be considered a prototype. As time goes on you will be improving the whole business; the product, the packaging, the marketing and distribution, the pricing, your team, and so on.

13. Celebrate little successes.

While keeping your eye on the long-term and medium-term goals, make sure you have short-term goals in the form of recognizable milestones. Celebrating your milestones is a good way of boosting your confidence and building your faith and momentum toward achieving the long-term goal. Make it a culture to celebrate your small successes.

14. Persist even if you fail.

There is no such thing as failure. When you are going somewhere and you find yourself on the wrong road, there is definitely something you can do. You can retrace your steps to the nearest recognizable junction and set yourself back on course, or trace a tangent from where you are to where you meet the right course or destination. You don't sit down and cry and say that you have failed to reach your destination. There are times when you take a wrong turn and wind up reaching your destination faster.

There are times when you take a wrong turn and it costs you time and effort to reach your destination, but by the time you get there you have harvested fruits along the way that make you richer upon arrival than you had anticipated. When people say you have failed, what they usually mean is that you have missed the attainment of a specific objective that was fixed for a specific time. Take note that this definition of failure holds in mostly artificial settings like a soccer match.

In real life, you can always revise objectives and time-frames as circumstances change, so long as you have a bigger goal. Even with a soccer match, the striker knows that the number of goals he scores depends on how many shots he takes to the goal post. He doesn't take the first shot, misses the target, gets disappointed and leaves the field. It is a very rare occurrence that a team wins a competition without having lost a match.

If you mix your cake and it doesn't come out well, you could as well make the best doughnuts for the time being, while you revise your knowledge on cake making to include the new lessons you just learned. Temporary defeat is not failure. It is feedback to tell you what is working and what is not working. Instead of getting emotional and feeling discouraged, be grateful for your temporary defeats and treat them as lessons that you should factor into your plan as you build a successful business.

Now you know that for you to be free from money worries, you must have a system that is making money for you while you are busy living the life you love. Building a money-making system means harnessing your super-powers with the money-making factors of human labor, commodities, services, assets, institutions, time, and markets, to come out with a model that you can multiply and sell where ever you are. Your personal wealth creation model is a seed that you can multiply as the need arises and as your market expands. Focus on having a seed of great value, because it is the value of the seed that will determine how far the business can expand.

Keep in mind that the money you make will always be a function of the number of people whose lives are served by your system. If you turn your model into a good business and grow it successfully, you can end up with a family business that you can pass down to your children, or a business you can sell on the stock market and retire if you want, or remain in it as CEO.

Bottom line is, once you have developed a valuable seed, there is no telling the limits to which it can expand when sown in the market. Just as you plant a seed, make other seeds out of the harvest and continue propagating your crop, your wealth creation model is something that you sow into the market and the market forces work in your favor to keep it expanding, so long as you keep cultivating it.

When you produce a good piece of music, you have built a wealth creation system. If it is a really good song that resonates with people, it will be propagated through social media and traditional media houses. The more people listen to your song, the more money you make. The more popular your song gets the more chances of your song being bought by advertising agencies and movie directors for use as soundtracks. As interest in you grows and your name becomes a marketable brand, you will start getting invitations to present at concerts, shows, and events.

A soft product like music can easily flow along the stream of the internet to entertain and inspire people in any part of the world. Thus, what you put in the seed, determines the size of your potential market.

If you are a local seamstress and you have noticed a growing interest in a certain clothing design among your clients, you can standardize and brand that design and put it in the market. With just a sewing machine and a few local fabrics, you can sit at home and produce an innovative design that appeals to thousands of people around the globe who are excited about reconnecting with their roots.

You may not have the resources to host expensive fashion shows, but you can host an inexpensive website through which you can showcase your designs to a wider audience than the possible number of people that could ever attend a live fashion show. With a few creative moves to sort out the issue of payments and shipping, you can have a fully functional business right from the comfort of your living room.

We are living in an age of open markets. Wealth is not a respecter of age, gender, culture, education, nationality, or religion. The only qualification you need on this earth to make money is your ability to think in terms of translating your superpowers into a product or service that serves as many people as possible.

You do not need any one's permission, so do not ask for anyone's permission. No one is an expert at it, so do not ask for permission. Seek out those who are doing what you want to do and place yourself under their mentorship. Apart from that, don't ask for peoples' opinion. Every new business is an invention. Innovation is never a product of book sense or advice. It is always a result of people infusing their authentic self into the circumstances they find themselves in and hatching out of it a unique solution that benefits people.

Irrespective of your financial goals, your freedom from the money hypnosis is the motive behind this venture of building your personal wealth creation system. It gives you the liberty to set your financial goal to the level that is convenient for you. The key is to earn the freedom that will enable you to spend your time the way you want, do the work you want, travel where you want, be with whom you want, and enjoy the quality of life you want, without worrying about money. Freedom to live your authentic life is your right, your prerogative, and in fact, your duty.

Do not make excuses why you should remain trapped in the illusion. The best excuse will not make life better for you. If you truly love yourself and are truly appreciative of this gift of life, then you will take the responsibility to live free and happy. Build for yourself a personal wealth creation system, and use it to get rich, while living your authentic life. This life is for you to live it. To be truly alive is to be fully awake.

GO AND DO SAME

The most important reasons why people do not achieve anything significant in their lives are as follows: they have no idea of what is possible for them, they lack clarity about what they really want, and they do not know how to go about achieving what they want. Before now, Cameroonians have been used to consuming success literature from America and other countries, often deriving little benefit from it because of many psychological barriers such as differences in context, inability to connect with the stories, difficulty in applying the theories, and a faulty self-image.

Now you have The Success Code that has been formulated by a Cameroonian from his Cameroonian experience. This Success Code has been explained to you using a success model, Pa Nangah, who started off as an ordinary Cameroonian kid, and attained godlike heights in professionalism, entrepreneurship, leadership, and philanthropy, in Cameroon.

People who know me know that I am sometimes very jovial and funny. But this book was not written for entertainment. God alone knows what I have been through to get this book in your hands, so I will conclude on a very serious note. I pray that in my lifetime I will see a thousand giants of the like of Pa Nangah arise from Cameroon and change the course of history. I do not care how this will happen. When Nangah was a poor boy in Mbatu village carrying firewood to Abakwa town with the rocks on the hilly foot paths tearing his bare feet, no one on earth knew that this kid would become a giant that would turn those same stones into architectural marvels.

If you have read this far, I am certain that you are feeling incredibly inspired. But I also know that it is not the first time you are feeling inspired or excited. You probably feel the same way each time you attend a good church service or a motivational seminar. Read this book over and over again. Every time you read, the words will not change but something will happen within you that did not happen the previous time. In fact, I suggest you never part with this book until you have achieved the purpose for which it was written, that is, until you have become the new Pa Nangah.

So here is the difference between excitement and inspiration. Fix in your mind a crystal clear vision of whom you want to become and what legacy you want to leave on this earth. Then find one inspired idea from this book that you are going to apply to your life every single day. If you do this, you would have turned excitement into inspiration and as you go along you will realize to your astonishment that people like Pa Nangah were not magicians. They were simply ordinary people that were living inspired lives. Listen to his voice that is now thundering in your head, "go and do same".

People are not limited by the place of their birth or by their surrounding circumstances, but by the size of their vision, the depth of their faith, and the creative work of their hands.

JOIN OUR COMMUNITY OF INSPIRED PEOPLE:

Share an inspiring story from your personal journey of self-transformation,

Write a review of this book,

Enroll for Godfrey's free mentorship program,

Subscribe to Godfrey's daily inspirational messages,

Shop for other books by Godfrey Esoh,

And much more.

Visit the website:

www.godfreyesoh.com

Please remember to write a review of this book on Amazon.com if you have not yet done so. Thank you.

www.ingramcontent.com/pod-product-compliance
Lightning Source LLC
Chambersburg PA
CBHW071512040426
42444CB00008B/1603